A HISTORY OF
COLLEGE
FOOTBALL
IN
GEORGIA

A HISTORY OF
COLLEGE
FOOTBALL
IN
GEORGIA

GLORY ON THE GRIDIRON

JON NELSON

FOREWORD BY **LORAN SMITH,**
WES DURHAM AND **NATE HIRSCH**

Charleston ——— London

THE
History
PRESS

Published by The History Press
Charleston, SC 29403
www.historypress.net

Cover images: bottom front image courtesy of Oglethorpe University Sports Information
Department; bottom back image courtesy of the Georgia Athletic Assocation.

First published 2012

Manufactured in the United States

ISBN 978.1.60949.694.4

Library of Congress CIP data applied for.

Notice: The information in this book is true and complete to the best of our knowledge. It is
offered without guarantee on the part of the author or The History Press. The author and
The History Press disclaim all liability in connection with the use of this book.

For Dad, I love you and I miss you…
and that will never change.

CONTENTS

FOREWORD

In discovering the history of college football in the state of Georgia, you find a lot of starts, stops, rebirths, second chances, stars and legends. For every century of work, there were other schools that tried just as hard, but all that's left are memories. I figured the best thing to do was defer to those who know what has happened on a few of those campuses. First, to Athens and Loran Smith. Loran, "Whaddyagot?"

In its illustrious history, which had its beginning in 1892, the University of Georgia has enjoyed multiple championships and honors. As the oldest chartered state university, Georgia was introduced to football by a chemist, Dr. Charles Herty, who invented the process for turning pine pulp into newsprint, thereby affecting the state forever. What has been more dominant to the state's image than the pine tree industry and football? And don't forget about Uga, ranked by *Sports Illustrated* as the nation's no. 1 mascot. Saturday afternoon between the hedges has been a must for Georgians, and others, for years. From the Rose Bowl to the Heisman Trophy, from the hedges to the chapel bell, Georgia is about tradition and a deep love of the Bulldogs with natives across the state. From Hahira to Brasstown Bald, from Tallapoosa to Tybee Light, the Red and Black has waved in the hearts and minds of loyal Georgians. From McWhorter to Sinkwich, Trippi, Sapp, Tarkenton, Herschel, Greene and Pollack; from Pop Warner to Butts, Dooley and Richt; and from championships in the SEC, the nation's toughest conference, to national championships, the university has a rich football heritage, playing its games in the most beautiful stadium imaginable. With an exciting campus built in the foothills of the Appalachians, the university's motto—to inquire into the nature of things—is a reminder that the first coach was also a scientist who gave equal emphasis to football and scholarship.

Now to the Flats and the voice of the Yellow Jackets, Wes Durham.

There are only a handful of football programs at the major college level that can compare with the history and tradition of Georgia Tech. Historically, the Yellow Jackets can lean on the coaching of John Heisman, Bill Alexander and Bobby Dodd. There have been national championship teams in varying generations, and this has also helped maintain the pride of the program. Then you have the players, the plays and the games that have helped define the nearly 120-year history of the Yellow Jackets. Tech fans will continue to discuss/argue as to who is the greatest player in their history. Is it Clint Castleberry or Calvin Johnson? Was the best team in 1952 or 1990? Was the greatest game the 1962 win over no. 1 Alabama or the 1990 win over no. 1 Virginia? Those moments, those debates, are what help to quantify one of the most consistent programs in the nearly 150-year history of college football.

Finally, our trip to Statesboro and Georgia Southern is addressed by one of the great voices of the Eagles, Nate Hirsch.

While Georgia Southern may have played football from 1924 to 1941, it's the modern era of the past thirty years that most fans remember. It all starts with a school president, Dr. Dale Lick, who had a vision. His original idea was to provide a school in south Georgia that gave athletes who couldn't play at Georgia or Georgia Tech an opportunity to continue playing football. The hiring of legendary coach Erk Russell changed everything. He sold the program to all of southeast Georgia. With an astute athletic director in Dr. David Wagner and the recruitment of some special players, including Tracy Ham, the Eagles not only made the playoffs but also won their first of six national championships in 1985. That team was special and repeated as national champs in 1986. Both the titles took place in Tacoma, Washington. What to do for an encore? In Erk's final season, you host the national championship game in Statesboro in 1989, go 15-0 and win the third title in front of a record overflow crowd of more than twenty-five thousand. More titles came in 1990, and then the Paul Johnson era produced a great player in Adrian

Peterson and two more titles in 1999 and 2000. What started as a vision back in 1980 has seen university status and enrollment grow, the latter from five thousand to more than twenty thousand, as well as continued success on the field. With current head coach Jeff Monken and his immediate success, the future looks bright at Georgia Southern.

Acknowledgements

Trying to knock out a project this size is like doing a "Greatest Hits" album (yes, I just dated myself). Hopefully, these pages will bring back memories for all of your schools and all of your teams that may be alive, dead or ready for a comeback in some form or another. First, the obvious thanks go to Jessica Berzon, Will McKay and everyone at The History Press for taking the idea and giving me the pleasure and privilege of making this happen. Saturdays are religious across the state of Georgia, and the churches are stadiums that range in seating size from a few hundred in the early days to almost 100,000 today. Everyone has their colors and sports them every other day of the week, 365 days a year. If you ask a fan about their team or their rival, be prepared for an earful in the positive or the negative.

For every part of the "good ol' days," there's just as much talk of the future. And for everyone who helped out with outright education, an interview, advice, photographs to help tell their own stories or proofreading of this manuscript to make sure everything is right, I can't thank all of you enough.

To my family—blood or otherwise—I can't thank you enough for seeing me to and through these deadlines. To the rest of the Outlaws, your calls are always treasured. To my mom, I love you and thank you for the mindset of an English major. To my dad, I know you're still watching.

Last and certainly not least: to Patty, the first two things I can say are that I have outkicked my coverage and that I am over my skis. I wouldn't have it any other way. Your unwavering support humbles me every moment of every day, and your love means the world to me.

And that's just the beginning; the word limit wouldn't even begin to cover it.

SPECIAL THANKS

Claude Felton and the University of Georgia.
Aimee Anderson, Dean Buchan and the folks at Georgia Tech.
Barrett Gilham and Georgia Southern University.
Andy Stabell and Mercer University.
Hoyt Young, Laura Masce and Oglethorpe University.
Mitch Gray and the University of West Georgia.
Bill Peterson, Matt Green, Phil Jones and Shorter University.
Shawn Reed and Valdosta State University.
Allison George and Georgia State University.
Rob Manchester, Bert Williams and Georgia Military College.
Paul Robards and Middle Georgia College.
Yusuf Davis and Morehouse College.
Dana Harvey and Clark Atlanta University.
Charles Ward and Fort Valley State University.
Debra Sloan and Georgia Southwestern University.
XOS Digital in Orlando, Florida.
Marcia Roberts for the help, Tommy Palmer for the reminders, Scott Singer, Mark Harmon for the sandwiches and sanity breaks, Loran Smith (who taught me how to write in a car without crashing it), Wes Durham, Nate Hirsch and all of the "Outlaws." You know who you are.

"Play it safe, everybody…we'll see you next time."

THE ABSOLUTE BEGINNINGS

It was the morning before college opened that I had my first sight of athletics at the University. Charles Ed Morris was standing under the shade of a large tree between the chapel and the Moore building, batting out flies to Cecil Wilcox, the Mell boys, and others, standing near the top of a high hill on the same elevation [as Old College]…Between the batters and the fielders was a deep gulch (I use the word advisedly). So steep was the decline from the outfield…that it was dangerous for the fielder to run forward on a fly ball and the ever-present small boy was utilized for returning to the batter the balls which fell short of the far outfield.

D r. Charles Herty wrote those words in the October 30, 1897 edition of the *Red and Black*, the on-campus newspaper at the University of Georgia (UGA), as he looked back on his days as an undergraduate thirteen years before. John F. Stegeman, the son of UGA coach and athletic director Herman Stegeman, quoted Herty in his own book *The Ghosts of Herty Field*.

Dr. Charles Herty came back to his alma mater to teach. Herty wanted to have a football game on campus in 1891, but he had to wait until the following year to have a contest with Macon's Mercer College.

Here's what the *Athens Banner* newspaper reported from the game:

The Mercer boys came in at twelve o'clock and brought with them two cars full of students and citizens of Macon, Madison, and other places along the line of the Macon and Northern. They were taken in charge by

The 1892 team photo. *Georgia Athletic Association.*

the University boys and entertained at their different homes…It was a fine delegation of young men and young ladies and a nicer crowd never came on a visit to Athens.

The University campus was decorated with black and crimson and on the field one goal was decorated with university colors, the other with Mercer colors. Long before three o'clock the crowd began to assemble and the yells of the two colleges were alternately raised with a vim by the boys. The university goat was driven across the field by the boys and raised quite a ripple of laughter. At three o'clock there were over one thousand people on the grounds, and the presence of so many ladies from the city, the Lucy Cobb [Institute] and the Home School, added inspiration to the occasion.

The Red and Black, as the Athens school was called in its early days, won the game, 50–0, on January 30, 1892. The next step, as is with athletics, was to start a rivalry that could unite the campus. The answer came from a Johns Hopkins classmate of Dr. Herty's, Dr. George Petrie at the Mechanical College of Alabama (now Auburn).

"Atlanta will be the scene Saturday of the first interstate intercollegiate football game," the *Atlanta Journal* reported on February 17, 1892. On the twentieth, in front of two thousand fans at Piedmont Park in Atlanta, Auburn beat Georgia, 10–0. The oldest rivalry in the Deep South was born.

Atlanta is one of many sites for the Auburn-Georgia rivalry. After playing the first ten games in Atlanta, the game had moved to Macon, Georgia, by 1904; Montgomery, Alabama, by 1908; and back into Georgia heading to Savannah after two Auburn straight wins.

In 1912, the game was moved between Atlanta and Athens before finding a permanent neutral site in the west Georgia town of Columbus. From 1916 to 1958, with the exception of 1929, when the two teams played in Athens, the Tigers and the Bulldogs met at McClung Memorial Stadium, where Georgia held a 22-16-2 advantage in the forty games on-site.

A HEAD COACH WITH POP

Herty, Earnest Brown (a graduate student who played and coached the team in 1893) and Robert Winston (the first paid coach at the university) all preceded a twenty-four-year-old who would make a name for himself and is still a name today: Glenn "Pop" Warner.

Warner graduated from Cornell with a law degree and had actually practiced law in Buffalo, New York, before taking the job in Athens for the 1895 ten-week season for $340. The team went 3-4, which was good enough for a $40-per week raise. The 1896 team followed up with an undefeated 4-0 mark. Warner would return to Ithaca, New York, by 1897. Charles McCarthy would succeed Warner and get credit for the first win over Georgia Tech, 28–0, in the 1897 season.

AND THEN IT ALMOST STOPPED

The state of Georgia can thank the mother of Vonalbade "Von" Gammon for having any kind of football. Period.

Von Gammon was a college player for the University of Georgia who died while playing a game against the University of Virginia on October 30, 1897. As a result, the Georgia House of Representatives passed a resolution the next day to ban football by a vote of ninety-one to three. The three college schools that played the sport at the time—Georgia, Georgia Tech and Mercer—all voluntarily disbanded their squads. The Georgia Senate followed with a vote outlawing football on November 18 by a margin of thirty-one to four. All Georgia governor William Atkinson needed to do was sign the resolutions into law, and football in the state would not exist.

However, Von Gammon's mother, Rosalind Burns Gammon, wrote a letter to her local representative:

> *It would be the greatest favor to the family of Von Gammon if your influence could prevent his death being used for an argument detrimental to the athletic cause and its advancement at the University. His love for his college and his interest in all manly sports, without which he deemed the highest type of manhood impossible, is well known by his classmates and friends, and it would be inexpressibly sad to have the cause he held so dear injured by his sacrifice. Grant me the right to request that my boy's death should not be used to defeat the most cherished object of his life. Dr. Herty's article in the Constitution of Nov. 2d is timely, and the authorities of the University can be trusted to make all needed changes for all possible consideration pertaining to the welfare of its students, if they are given the means and the confidence their loyalty and high sense of duty should deserve.*

When Governor Atkinson was made aware of the letter and Mrs. Gammon's feelings on the matter, he didn't sign the resolution. The University of Georgia was presented a plaque by the surviving members of that 1897 University of Virginia team in 1921, and Rosalind Gammon is credited for saving the sport.

If you ever visit Gammon's hometown of Rome, there is a memorial plaque embedded in the sidewalk outside Jefferson's restaurant at the corner of Broad and East Fourth Streets telling the tale and reminding us all of a selfless act in a time of grief.

THE WORLD'S LARGEST WHATEVER IT'S CALLED

Georgia actually first played Florida on October 15, 1904, in Macon, Georgia, with the Bulldogs defeating the Gators, 52–0. Florida doesn't recognize that game as official. But Georgia does.

The Bulldogs wouldn't meet the Gators again until 1915 in Jacksonville. That game was a big deal for the city back then. Jacksonville's mayor, J.E.T. Bowden, declared the Friday before the game a "half" holiday for local business. Georgia would prevail in the 1915 game, 37–0.

It would be eighteen years before the Georgia-Florida game would find a permanent site. The game moved around from Tampa in 1919 to Athens, Gainesville and even Savannah, Georgia, which hosted the game in 1928.

THE FIRST ALL-AMERICAN

Bob McWhorter was five feet, eight inches tall and weighed in at a rock-solid 190 pounds. "Stop McWhorter" became a rallying cry of a lot of schools between 1910 and 1914 as he was one of the hardest backs to bring down in his time. He would be part of the class that could say that, during its time, it beat Georgia Tech and Alabama four times while splitting the four games with Auburn. There was also talk that, after his graduation at Georgia, as he pursued a law degree at the University of Virginia, McWhorter (or someone who looked a lot like him) played under an alias in Charlottesville.

THE EARLY TWENTIETH CENTURY

THE RED AND BLACK TURNS BULLDOGS

The university's founder and first president, Abraham Baldwin, was a Yalie, and its mascot is a white English bulldog. Baldwin even modeled the UGA campus after Yale College's for its official opening in 1801 after its initial, sixteen-year planning phase.

But most of the attribution for the nickname "Bulldogs" and an association with the University of Georgia starts in November 1920. Morgan Blake of the *Atlanta Journal* newspaper thought that the "Georgia Bulldogs" would "sound good because there is a certain dignity about a bulldog, as well as ferocity." Three days later, after a scoreless tie played against the University of Virginia, *Atlanta Constitution* writer Cliff Wheatley used the term a handful of times in an article, and the nickname has stayed ever since.

It could have been something else entirely. Georgia was simply known as the "Red and Black," the traditional colors, and there is also the story about a goat hanging around in the early days of the program as a frequent spectator from the sidelines. But thankfully, no one has pictures or proof.

So "Bulldogs" will just have to do. Could you imagine the Georgia "G" standing for "Goats"?

THE ROARING TWENTIES IN ATHENS

Under W.A. Cunningham, the Red and Black had their first solid run of winning seasons—seven of eight in the decade of the 1910s. H.J. Stegeman played for Amos Alonzo Stagg at the University of Chicago and took over for Cunningham in 1920. His four years would yield an SIAA title in the first year, when the team went 8-0-1, and three more successful seasons before he turned over coaching to 1911 Georgia captain George "Kid" Woodruff for the 1923 season. Woodruff was already a successful businessman in the town of Columbus, so he only took one dollar per year to run the program. Two assistants on the staff came from Knute Rockne's Notre Dame sideline—backs coach Frank Thomas and line coach Harry Mehre—and they would introduce the Irish formation to southern football.

The crowning glory of the Woodruff tenure was a national championship in 1927, even after a 12-0 season-ending loss to Georgia Tech. The "Dream and Wonder Team," led by ends Chick Shiver

"Kid" Woodruff. *Georgia Athletic Association.*

22

and all-American Tom Nash, registered six shutouts, including one at Yale in New Haven, and could even take credit for the first win ever at Legion Field in Birmingham, beating Alabama. The loss to Georgia Tech prevented Georgia from winning even the Southern Conference title, as North Carolina State went 4-0 and Tennessee went 5-0-1, but the Bulldogs would still be awarded the title by one national poll at the end of the year. The game against Tech had to be held in Atlanta for the eighteenth time in a row since it was determined that Sanford Field (or any other place in Athens) was "inadequate." University president Steadman Sanford was so disgusted at losing to the Golden Tornado that he made sure that his school would have its own facility worth playing in from then on.

Two years later, in the same month of the stock market crash, the stadium bearing his name was christened, with a special touch surrounding it.

THE HEDGES EMERGE

So how did the "Hedges" come to be that all-important signature to Sanford Stadium?

Back in 1929, President Steadman Sanford wanted the "best football stadium in Dixie." Charlie Martin, who held most every job in the athletic program at some point, had seen the roses at the Rose Bowl in 1926 and thought that the flower would be a good idea.

One problem: roses wouldn't last, so they settled on hedges, which were installed just hours before the Georgia Bulldogs–Yale game on October 12, 1929, which UGA won, 15–0. Vernon "Catfish" Smith scored all fifteen points that day to cement his place in Bulldog lore.

More than thirty thousand fans showed up for the game itself, and nine southern governors were also in attendance. Coach Dan Magill says it was the biggest athletic event to be held in the South at the time. As the story goes, Grantland Rice, the legendary sportswriter who spent time at the *Atlanta Journal* in his early years, was the first to use a popular phrase. According to Magill, Rice said that Georgia would "have its opponent between the hedges" when describing one game in Athens.

Steadman Sanford. *Georgia Athletic Association.*

"Whence Cometh that Bear?"

Mercer's "Bears" nickname even came from a University of Georgia player in that first contest when, as a Macon player was running with the football, a Red and Black player allegedly exclaimed the phrase.

Mercer alumnus Steadman Sanford himself told that story as to the beginnings of the nickname. After its loss to Georgia in 1892, the school played unsanctioned ball for a while. After the near elimination of the sport following the death of Von Gammon, the Bears didn't resume the sport until 1903, and only as long as the players who participated wouldn't have any more than two unexcused absences in classes. The sport almost disappeared again, with the lone game on the schedule being a 50–0 loss to Georgia Tech. Had the contract not been fulfilled, there would have been a $1,000 forfeit to the home team. The matchup seemed to be a surprise to the campus, as the Bears didn't have a coach or any players, and the next game with Georgia was cancelled because of the result.

The first "paid" football coach for Mercer was E.E. Tarr in 1906, and the "Tarros" played a six-game schedule and added another team to their group of "firsts." Mercer shut out the Florida Gators each of the first five times the universities met, with the Bears winning the first four, 12–0, 6–0, 24–0 and 13–0, and the teams tying in 1912, 0–0.

The team seemed to have turned a corner by 1910 with the hiring of Dr. C.C. Stroud from the University of Rochester as the "Director of Physical Culture" in addition to coaching and teaching history. He had led his old squad to three titles up north and got the Bears to a 6-3 finish in his first year on the sidelines. But Stroud left after the 1912 season to become track coach at Louisiana State University (LSU). The Bears surrendered 105 points in 1914 to Tech, but the "Battling Baptists," as Robert Wilder referred to them in his book *Gridiron Glory Days: Football at Mercer, 1892–1942*, kept playing even without a real budget and a student body big enough to match the southern schools on their schedules.

FOOTBALL ON NORTH AVENUE

The third member of the nineteenth-century football club was the Golden Tornado of the Georgia Institute of Technology in Atlanta. Mercer would also be the answer to a trivia question where the Golden Tornado are concerned. The following fall after debuting with Georgia in Athens, Mercer played Georgia Tech at Central City Park in Macon, winning 12–6 in Tech's first-ever college football game. In 1894, Captain Leonard Wood was a stalwart of the squad since there were no real eligibility rules. He was recognized as one of the legends of the service as an army surgeon and eventually reached the rank of major general.

In 1904, the school hired the coach of Clemson University away from the state of South Carolina. John Heisman made his name in college football at Oberlin College in Ohio, Buchtel College (now the University of Akron), the Agricultural and Mechanical College of Alabama (Auburn University) in 1895–99 and Clemson. Heisman became the first paid coach in college football history, according to some, earning $2,250 and 30 percent of the gate receipts from home games.

Tech went 2-5 the year before but turned it around to 8-1-1 in 1904. Tech would not have a losing season under Heisman's tutelage. His last

John Heisman. *Georgia Tech Athletic Association.*

five teams, before Heisman returned north in 1920, were 37-4-2 and included a thirty-three-game winning streak during which Tech outscored its opponents 1,599 to 99—an average of a little better than 48-3.

But one of the biggest moments for the young program came on October 7, 1916, in a game against Cumberland University of Lebanon, Tennessee. The year before, CU brought in professional baseball players for a win over Tech, and the game stuck with fans and alums so much that they wanted revenge. Head football coach John Heisman offered the school a $500 guarantee to come down for a football game. The Golden Tornado averaged almost ten yards per carry, never picking up a first down (because they scored on every possession before needing a change of yardsticks). Cumberland didn't get a first down, either, mainly because it was heading backward, and was led by all-American Everett Strupper's six touchdowns.

Coach Heisman actually fielded two entire teams for the game that played alternating quarters. Heisman promised a steak dinner to the team that scored the most points. At halftime, Tech led 126–0; each team had scored 63 points. Forty years later, the two teams organized a reunion. According to alumni releases from the Tech side, Heisman wasn't done with the visitors up 126 points.

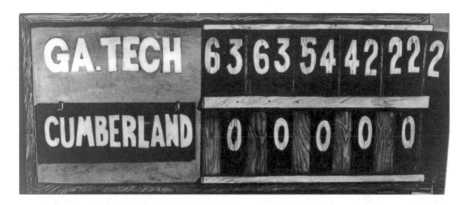

The scoreboard never lies. *Georgia Tech Athletic Association.*

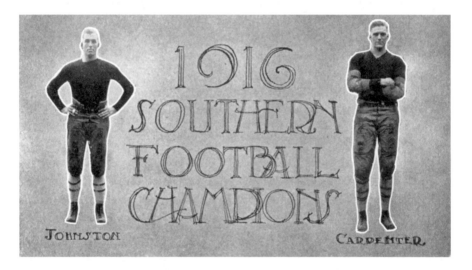

The Golden Tornado's 1916 handiwork. *Georgia Tech Athletic Association.*

"You're doing all right, team," Heisman told his players in a rousing halftime pep talk. "We're ahead. But you just can't tell what those Cumberland players have up their sleeves. They may spring a surprise. Be alert, men! Hit 'em clean, but hit 'em hard!" At the game's end, Heisman decided that both Tech teams had earned steak dinners.

Sportswriter Grantland Rice, who witnessed the contest, reported, tongue firmly in cheek, "Cumberland's greatest individual play of the game occurred when fullback Allen circled right for a six-yard loss." For the record, the Bulldogs didn't resume football until 1920. Heisman followed up the Cumberland massacre with a title run the following year.

The 1917 national championship squad is viewed in some circles as being greater than the "Four Horsemen" of Notre Dame and just shy of the 1945 Army squad as the best ever backfield. With Everett Strupper and "Big Chief" Joe Guyon, the Tornado ran over, around and through every opponent. Heisman's team had victories of 98–0 over Carlisle, 68–7 over Auburn and 48–0 over Tulane and employed some new wrinkles in the game that evolved into staples of the modern-day sport: the center snap, the "jump" shift and the forward pass. It even impressed one of the premier athletes of the late nineteenth century. "That jump shift is about the slickest offense I ever saw," said Billy Sunday. "I want to tell you that I've seen all the great Harvard and Princeton teams in action, but never one as great as this team of Tech."

But as good as the title team was in 1917, the First World War leaves historians wondering what could have been in 1918. Guyon would return with only two others on offense. Strupper would enter the U.S. Navy, and two freshmen, Buck Flowers and Red Barron, would star for a team that would put up some impressive numbers against inexperienced and thin squads: 128–0 over North Carolina State and 118–0 over Furman.

When Heisman left, one of his players took over the coaching. The pride of Mud River, Kentucky, William Alexander, played for Heisman in the 1911 and 1912 seasons, graduated with a degree in civil engineering and was valedictorian of his class. The impact Alexander had on the field was immediate, with two straight SIAA titles, a Southern Conference title and a 23-4 start. The *Technique* newspaper sensed a change after the transition to Alexander: "Since Coach Alex has taken charge there is a change in the team. The youngest coach in major football, he is probably the most popular, and bids fair to prove himself the peer of them all. Not only is Coach the idol of members of the team, but of the student body as well."

Another SoCon title in 1927 was followed by the school's second national title in 1928. The 10-0 season for Alexander got a little help from someone who went the wrong way.

In the second quarter of its game with Cal, Tech's J.C. "Stumpy" Thomason fumbled at the Golden Bear thirty-yard line after a hit from Benny Lom. Cal co-captain Roy Riegels picked up the ball, got some blocking and spun out of trouble. The problem was that Riegels was

The first Tech all-American, Everett Strupper. *Georgia Tech Athletic Association.*

The "Golden" 1928 squad. *Georgia Tech Athletic Association.*

"Wrong Way" Riegels at the Rose Bowl. *Georgia Tech Athletic Association.*

heading in reverse. Lom was tracking Riegels down, yelling, "Stop, stop! You're running the wrong way!" Riegels replied as Lom tried to get him moving in the other direction, "Get away from me! This is my touchdown." Lom eventually got Riegels heading back in the right direction at the Cal three-yard line after the failed first attempt at the ten. Tech tackled Riegels at the one. Cal tried to punt out of trouble on the first play after the wrong-way run with Riegels snapping to Lom, but Tech's Vance Maree blocked the punt and it rolled out of bounds for a safety. The play eventually made the difference in the 8–7 win.

After the play, Riegels was inundated by mail that included a marriage proposal, sponsorship of upside-down cakes, a backward walkathon and a necktie with stripes running the wrong way.

Interviewed by *Sports Illustrated* in 1955, Riegels had accepted his place in college football history. "I used to be sensitive," he says, "but everybody else thought it was funny and I finally decided that all I could do was laugh with them. Sometimes my 10-year-old son calls me 'Wrong Way Riegels'—and I don't even spank him for it."

WHAT EXACTLY IS A STORMY PETREL?

Submitted on May 15, 1935, Oglethorpe University head football coach John Patrick finished his master's thesis. It was titled "Football at Oglethorpe University: A History," and in its sixty-five pages, complete with a nine-page introduction, Patrick chronicled his Petrels' ups-and-downs from their beginnings eighteen years earlier and traced the sport of football to the Greek sport "harpaston" and the Italian version "calcio."

Frank Anderson, after two weeks of practice in 1917, brought out the first Petrels squad that beat Georgia Fifth District A&M, 18–0, for their first-ever win. Bill Johnson scored the first touchdown in school history, but the first decade on Peachtree Road in Atlanta would have both highs and lows. A 55–0 Camp Gordon loss in 1918 was at the hands of Everett Strupper (yes, Tech's Everett Strupper), and the 1919 team beat Mercer in Atlanta, 73–0, and the University of Florida, 14–7, on Thanksgiving. They would travel three thousand miles and only play one home game, but they were building their reputation of taking on all comers. Woolworth's executive Harry Hermance even pledged at the 1919 football banquet that

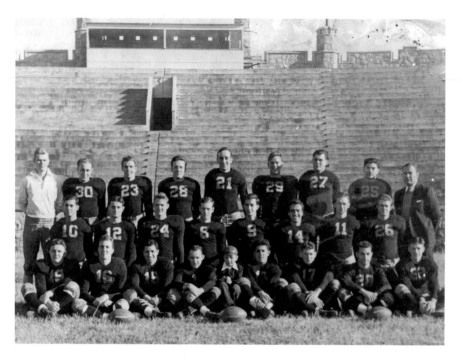

The Stormy Petrels in their playing days. *Oglethorpe University Sports Information Department.*

he would be in charge of raising $5,000 a year over the next ten years to help Oglethorpe build a premier football stadium.

Under the Robertson brothers, first Jim and then Harry, starting in 1923, Oglethorpe won back-to-back Southern Intercollegiate Athletic Association titles, going 6-3-1 and 8-3 in '24 and '25. But there were two signature wins for the school. The first was in the 1926 season. The Stormy Petrels finished 3-6-1 after their second SIAA title, but a 7–6 win on the Flats over Georgia Tech was a bigger score for the school as their flag was raised in victory.

From Patrick's thesis:

> *The boys labored under the hot September sun, but it was not in vain. Oglethorpe defeated Georgia Tech 7-6. "Cy" Bell, the great halfback, broke loose on a fake reverse play that took the Yellow Jackets unexpected, and raced 42 yards for a touchdown. "Nutty" Campbell kicked the extra point that spelled defeat for Georgia Tech. The Petrels went wild, they had beaten Tech after six years of trying.*

Three seasons later, the next win for the program that gave the school added southern legitimacy was against the Red and Black in a year that finished up 5-4-1.

Again from Patrick:

> *Since the beginning of football at Oglethorpe, the dream of all Petrel football aspirants has been to beat Georgia and Georgia Tech, having accomplished the latter in 1926, by the tune of 7–6. The Petrels came back this year and won over their master and big brother, and when the battle ended, the score was Georgia 7, Oglethorpe 13. "Cy" Bell broke through off tackle and raced sixty four yards for the winning touchdown.*

Ed Danforth of the *Atlanta Constitution* was just as lyrical in his description of the game winner: "If a man may be his own ghost, 'old' Cy was the wraith of the young Cy Bell who galloped through the Georgia Tech team in 1926 back in Atlanta and beat the Mighty Engineers 7 to 6. Cy, the Giant Killer!—to have scored the touchdown that beat two supposedly mightier foes, is a thrilling experience that comes to few halfbacks who wear the livery of a small college."

In 1929, Harry Hermance revealed that he was responsible for the $50,000 funding of the first stage of the football stadium construction. The stadium was named in his honor in a victory over the University of Dayton. The stadium has remained one-quarter finished to this day, as Hermance lost his entire fortune three days after the dedication due to the stock market crash.

By the end of the decade, however, Oglethorpe President Thornwell Jacobs was becoming less and less enthused over what athletics was turning into—more business than sport. In his autobiography, relayed by Paul Stephen Hudson's article "Flight of the Stormy Petrel: The Glory Years of Oglethorpe University Athletics" in *Atlanta History* magazine in the summer of 1992, Jacobs felt athletics was "at once the bane and blessing of the American college: the bane because it is the source of anxiety and trouble, the blessing because it is the source of more pleasure, college spirit, and money than all other sources of student activity combined."

And that's still a feeling fairly popular today. Jacobs was more inclined to have academics in charge of the athletic program and even wanted his athletic directors to be faculty members. The expense of a program and

The Hermance family at the Oglethorpe Stadium dedication. *From Thornwell Jacobs's* Step Down, Dr. Jacobs: The Autobiography of an Autocrat *(Westminster Publishers, 1945).*

his disappointment of the system had caused him to scale back his own program by the 1930s, when his football team hovered around .500 rather than challenge for conference titles. By 1943, athletics was suspended for the Second World War, and the sport of football never returned to campus.

These days, the Stormy Petrels' successes are in basketball and baseball, but if you look hard enough, you'll see T-shirts around campus supporting Oglethorpe football: "Undefeated Since 1940."

A "MEHRE" SUCCESS

The Bulldogs continued their on-the-field work in the 1930s, with Harry Mehre as head coach, with seven of his eight teams in the decade finishing above .500, being in contention for the Southern and Southeastern Conference titles and even beating the feared Yale team for five straight seasons.

But as with most fervent fans, when national championships are part of the history, the desire is to reclaim that past glory. In his 3,693-page *History of the University of Georgia*, Thomas Walter Reed summed this up in his review of the 1934 season: "The season of 1934 was satisfactory with seven wins and three losses and 141 points to 56 for the opponents. But it marked the beginning of a slow slide downward until 1941, two years after Wallace Butts came as coach, since which time the Red and Black has turned in remarkable performances including four bowl games."

And after the last of the five wins in a row over Yale, Reed continued with his assessment of a school that had, perhaps, had enough of a north/south rivalry: "Yale has not appeared on the Georgia schedule since that game. Perhaps the Yale football warriors came to the conclusion that they had had enough of Georgia to last for a time at least."

The 6-3-2 season of Mehre in 1937 was the last chapter in his book in Athens. He had served on campus for fourteen years, ten of them as head coach. Alumni had decided that it was time for a change. Some wanted to keep Mehre around in some capacity, but the majority drowned out that thought process. At the end-of-the-year football banquet hosted by the Athens Rotary Club, Mehre simply said that for the betterment of the team and the program he should "sever his relationship." He moved to Oxford, Mississippi, to coach Ole Miss and took assistant Weems Baskin with him. Assistants Rex Enright, Ted Twomey and "Catfish" Smith moved over to South Carolina, with Enright as head coach.

The new guy only lasted a year. Joel Hunt, an assistant at LSU and a star at Texas A&M, was the surprise pick to replace Mehre. His assistants were Elmer Lampe, J.V. Sikes and Wallace Butts. And after a 5-4-1 year, Butts was elevated to the top spot. The Hunt tenure is thought of as more a bump in the road, soon to be forgotten. The 1939 season turned into a "mulligan" for the fans as they saw something in Butts's coaching that could return the team to past glories. They would be right.

The year 1939 was a fantastic one for the Yellow Jackets as well, with their win in the Orange Bowl over Missouri to put a wrap on an 8-2 record and a co-champion marker in the Southeastern Conference. The season started with a loss to second-ranked Notre Dame in South Bend. A loss to twelfth-ranked Duke put Coach Alexander's squad at 3-2, but wins over top-twenty opponents Kentucky, Alabama, Florida and Georgia put the team in Miami to play the sixth-ranked Tigers at Roddy Burdine Stadium (the name of the stadium before it, too, was referred to as the Orange Bowl).

Johnny Bosch, all 147-pounds of him, led Tech to 21 unanswered points after "Passing Paul" Christman gave Missouri a 7-0 lead. The game was also the beginning of the storied writing career of Edwin Pope. As an eleven-year-old living in Athens, Pope listened to the radio broadcast of Ted Husing and kept a running account of the game. He took his typed story the next day to the *Athens Banner Herald*.

"I asked if they wanted to use the running story of the Georgia Tech–Missouri game," Pope remembered when he was interviewed for his induction into the College Football Hall of Fame in 2000. "They said no. But they asked me, 'Did you type this? Do you want a job?' They put me to work covering small sports. When I was 12 and 13, I covered high school sports. When I was 15, they made me the sports editor of the paper and I was covering the University of Georgia. I was the youngest sports editor in the nation."

Nothing like Georgia Tech giving someone living in Athens their start in the business…

Mercer Tries Again

The Macon school resumed football in 1919 after taking a hiatus for World War I. Josh Cody was hired as coach during the early 1920s, and former Tech all-American Strupper joined the staff as an assistant, coaching the backs. After a 5-6 year in 1922, he moved on to Vanderbilt and Strupper resigned. Stanley Robinson became the fourteenth coach in the thirty-one-year history of the program after a successful run at Mississippi College, and he went 4-5, 5-3-2 (including winning 5 of 6) and 4-5. Bernie Moore followed with three near-.500 seasons of his own before moving to LSU himself.

The 1927 team had two of the most well-known names in Bears history: Wally Butts, who made his name in Athens (later on in this book), and running back "Phoney" Smith. Smith had such an impact on the program that the Armistice Day/"Dad's Day" game on November 11, 1927, was also called "Phoney Smith Day." He led the Bears to a 21–6 win over Oglethorpe with 159 yards rushing. Fellow alum and future University of Georgia legend Wally Butts had extraordinary praise for "Phoney" in 1966: "Phoney Smith should be in the National Hall of Fame. Bernie Moore should be able to assist. Please get this idea started and count on me for help. At one time *I could have done the job*."

Moore moved on to LSU after the 1928 season, giving way to Lake Russell, who came in from Carson-Newman. Moore also played an important role with one of Mercer's rival schools, Georgia Tech, when he was in charge of the Southeastern Conference. Russell took the reins of the Macon program until the war.

The 1931 team went 6-3, with only three home games on the schedule since, apparently, too many passes were given out and the home games lost money. The 6-2 1932 squad even drew the praise of *Atlanta Constitution* sports editor Ralph McGill, as he proclaimed, "It is difficult for me to understand how Mercer's team could be as strong as it was during the season considering the fact that material was scanty and that equipment was not on par with other schools." Five players were given All-Dixie Conference status, and three (Lester Olsson, Bob Smith and Ernie Zinkowski) were named First Team SIAA.

By 1933, Olsson had picked up All-SIAA, All-Dixie and honorable mention all-American honors and was recognized as one of the school's best linemen ever. He was the only Mercer player in history to play in the NFL, with the Washington Redskins. Russell ended his tenure after the 1940 season with a career coaching mark of 43-60-5 in his twelve years. Wilder addressed the idea of Russell sticking it out as long as he did in Macon in his *Gridiron Glory Days* book:

> *Russell was actually a victim of the times. He came to Mercer during the depression of 1929 and stayed through some financially difficult years for the athletic program and for the University. It took a considerable amount of courage to return each year to be faced with the same problems: lack of money, personnel, and support by the fans at the box office.*

And the end was nearing.

THE 1940s

On December 3, 1940, the administration at Mercer decided that it was going to get out of the football business. But fifteen days later, the decision was reversed by the board of trustees after a great deal of discussion and disagreement. The sport, however, would be "de-emphasized" and the school would enter the South Atlantic Athletic Conference with Wofford, Newberry, Presbyterian, Oglethorpe, Stetson and Rollins. The 1941 team went 3-6, but off-season discussions about the budget, scholarships and the large amount of unpaid bills the team had accrued made the relationship between the athletic department and administration somewhat testy. World War II ended up being the ultimate decider as the program was suspended for the duration of the war on January 7, 1942.

In 1946, university president Dr. Spright Dowell was presented with a proposal to resurrect the program. Dowell wasn't a fan of "big-time" football or subsidizing athletes more than the university's student body itself. He had no objection to having non-scholarship athletes participating, but anything else was unacceptable. Other sports would work under that premise, Dowell thought, but in an executive committee meeting of the trustees in February, he told them that he would rather retire if it meant a solution to the problem.

Dowell didn't need to retire, and Mercer stayed without football…for a while.

Unfortunately, Mercer would have to wait. *Mercer University Sports Information Department.*

THE BEST BACKFIELD EVER?

Head Coach Wally Butts had been steadily upgrading the talent on the Georgia Bulldog football team throughout the late 1930s and early 1940s. Frank Sinkwich became a Georgia Bulldog legend. But if it hadn't been for a chance stop at an Ohio gas station, history might have been different. Back in the summer of 1939, backfield coach Bill Hartman was on a recruiting trip in Ohio that didn't go well, at least initially.

Hartman made the long car trip from Athens to Youngstown, Ohio, to recruit someone the coaches thought was the best back in Ohio. When Hartman arrived, he was too late. That particular back was heading to Ohio State. On his way back into town, Hartman stopped at a gas station to fill up and struck up a conversation with the attendant, who told him that the best back in Ohio lived a few blocks down the road. It was Frank Sinkwich.

Sinkwich was a star athlete at Chaney High School in Youngstown, where he played running back. Hartman got some boys together to see Sinkwich for himself and discovered what the gas station attendant was talking about. The coaching staff knew that Sinkwich could be a special player and would do anything to convince him to play for the Bulldogs. All

Frank Sinkwich. *Georgia Athletic Association.*

Sinkwich asked was that his friend and teammate George Poschner receive a scholarship as well. It was a done deal. But Poschner almost never made it to school in Athens—his high school transcript had too many vocational credits, and it took the registrar's office debating the high school class load that would eventually allow him in.

Sinkwich and the rest of Georgia's freshman football team (the "Bullpups") scored at will and became known as the "Point-a-Minute-Bullpups." After an unbeaten freshman season, Sinkwich moved to the varsity team that had gone 5-6 the year before.

Sinkwich started slowly as a sophomore. Coach Butts decided to go with experience for the season opener against Oglethorpe, and Sinkwich only carried the ball once for 15 yards. The next week against South Carolina, Sinkwich ran for two long touchdowns and threw for another. After strong performances against Columbia and Kentucky, Sinkwich was finally inserted into the Bulldogs' starting lineup in November against Auburn; he threw a touchdown pass. He ended his sophomore season with a great game against Georgia Tech. A few days before the game, Sinkwich was laid up in his dorm room with a high fever, but against the Yellow Jackets he showed no effects—running for 128 yards on twenty-eight carries and throwing for a pair of touchdowns as the Bulldogs defeated the Jackets, 21–19. Until then, Georgia's last win over Georgia Tech was back in 1936. UGA won the next week over Miami, and the Bulldogs ended the 1940 season 5-4-1.

Much was expected from Sinkwich for the 1941 season, and those expectations were met, but not without some difficulties. In Georgia's second game of the year against South Carolina, Sinkwich ran into Gamecock end Steve Novak, who gave the Georgia back a hard lick to the jaw. Then, late in the game, while Sinkwich ran out of bounds, he took a late hit to the jaw again. Years later, when asked, Sinkwich thought that the second hit was from Novak as well, but that hit out of bounds knocked him out of the game—even so, he didn't miss any other games during the season.

Team dentist Dr. Jerry Allen wired Sinkwich's jaw shut for the next game against Ole Miss. A local machinist made a metal chinstrap for protection. Sinkwich ran for 98 yards and threw a touchdown as the Bulldogs and Rebels ended in a 14–14 tie. Against Columbia, Sinkwich received a special helmet with a large jaw protector attached that he wore for the remainder of the 1941 season. Sinkwich ran for a then SEC record 1,103 yards and also set the SEC total offense record with 2,187 yards. Sinkwich led the Bulldogs to a 9-1-1 record and UGA's first postseason bowl game: the Orange Bowl against Texas Christian University (TCU) on New Year's Day 1942.

In front of 35,786 fans (an attendance record at the time), Sinkwich went 9 for 13, passing for 243 yards and three touchdowns and added another score with a 43-yard touchdown run in the third quarter. By the end of the day, Sinkwich accounted for 382 yards of total offense with four touchdowns as the Bulldogs routed TCU, 40–26. His year earned him all-American honors and a fourth-place finish in the Heisman Trophy voting. However, his Orange Bowl performance got Sinkwich noticed outside the Southeast.

Even though Sinkwich shared the offensive load with his understudy, Charley Trippi, his senior season was another great year. Georgia went on to an 11-1 season and, with a 34–0 victory over archrival Georgia Tech to close the season, received a bid to the Rose Bowl to take on the University of California–Los Angeles (UCLA). Playing on two sprained ankles, he scored the only touchdown of the game as Georgia defeated UCLA, 9–0, to finish 11-1 and win the program's first national championship.

For the 1942 season, Frank Sinkwich rushed for 742 yards, passed for 1,392 yards and scored twenty-four total touchdowns. Sinkwich earned all-American honors and won the Heisman Trophy by unanimous vote, becoming the first southern football player to win that award.

"Fireball Frankie," as he was called, had a secret: flat feet. Ed Danforth of the *Atlanta Journal* said of Sinkwich that "his feet were so flat that the ROTC instructor at the University of Georgia refused him for military training his freshman year. Yet Fritz Lutz, the Bulldog trainer, says those same very flat feet gave Frankie the traction to cut at full speed, something few backs could do." Sinkwich moved to South Carolina after graduation and was in and out of military service because of those flat feet and bad ankles. His no. 21 jersey was retired following that season—the first Georgia Bulldog so honored.

Sinkwich was the first pick of the 1943 NFL draft, for the Detroit Lions. He was named all-pro as a rookie in 1943 and 1944, along with getting the NFL's MVP, but his playing career ended there. Sinkwich returned to Athens in the late 1940s where he became a beer distributor and a major supporter of the Georgia Bulldogs. Sinkwich and his former coach Bill Hartman chaired the committee that raised funds for the construction of Butts-Mehre Heritage Hall, which was completed in 1987.

Sinkwich died of cancer on October 22, 1990.

WHEN SINKWICH DIDN'T RUN THE BALL

Georgia was led by seniors George Poschner, who earned all-American honors at end of that year, and freshman Charley Trippi, giving Georgia one of the most potent offenses in the country in 1942.

The Bulldogs opened the 1942 season in Louisville, Kentucky, against the Kentucky Wildcats and held on to win, 7–6. From then on, the Bulldogs cruised with double-digit wins over Jacksonville NAS, Furman, Ole Miss, Tulane and Cincinnati. Georgia was ranked number two in the nation heading into a showdown with third-ranked Alabama. The Bulldogs and the Crimson Tide met at Grant Field on the Georgia Tech campus in Atlanta on October 31, 1942. With World War II raging in Europe and the South Pacific, fuel rationing was in effect, so Atlanta was the neutral site.

It had been thirteen years since Georgia had defeated Alabama. But in the fourth quarter, down 10–0, a pass from Sinkwich to Poschner from five yards out cut the lead to 10–7. Later in the fourth, the Bulldogs had a second and eleven on the Alabama fifteen-yard line. Sinkwich found Poschner again, and as he caught the ball, Poschner was hit high and low and was flipped upside down. He came down on his head but held on, and those who saw it say that Poschner caught the ball "standing on his head." Georgia had the lead, 14–10, and Poschner's catch went down in Georgia Bulldog lore, as they went on to win, 21–10. "You're the greatest bunch of battlers I have ever seen," Coach Butts told his players after the Alabama win.

The following Monday, Georgia was ranked number one in the nation. The Bulldogs went on to destroy the Florida Gators, 75–0, and UT-Chattanooga, 40–0, on the road. The roll would end on a late November afternoon in Columbus, Georgia, against Auburn. The Bulldogs were beaten by the Tigers, 27–13, for their only loss of the season. Georgia went from number one to number five for their showdown with second-ranked Georgia Tech in Athens.

The 1942 Georgia–Georgia Tech game winner would have a shot at the national championship, as the day before the game, the Rose Bowl committee announced that the winner of that match would be invited to play UCLA on New Year's Day 1943 in Pasadena. Thousands of extra seats were added in Sanford Stadium to see Georgia rout Georgia Tech, 34–0, to earn the shot at the national championship.

After the game, Georgia was declared the national champion in six polls recognized by the National Collegiate Athletic Association (NCAA) at that time: DeVold, Houlgate, Litkenhous, Williamson, Poling and Berryman.

A Distinguished Career

Poschner's story didn't end in Athens. He was wounded by a bullet to the face during the Allied maneuvers in the Battle of the Bulge, but because of the brutally cold conditions, he didn't die. He was taken back to a hospital, where he had his legs amputated, and he spent years recovering in veterans facilities in the States. He attended games in his wheelchair in Athens when he could and was awarded the Purple Heart, Bronze Star and Distinguished Service Cross.

"When he was down and out at Walter Reed Hospital [in Washington, D.C.], guys tried to get him to accept it. Eventually, he softened and realized it was the life he'd have to lead," his brother-in-law, Emil Basista, said in a 2004 interview with the *Youngstown Vindicator* newspaper's John Bassetti. Poschner was quoted as saying, "I learned to accept it a long time ago. God has kept me alive for a certain purpose and I've got to see if I can do what He wants." And he did it with the original bucket-strap limbs, despite the technological advances that would come along over time. The originals were good enough for him.

In 1982, Sinkwich said that "knowing George has made me stronger all my life" at a testimonial dinner in his hometown of Youngstown, Ohio. That same year, Sinkwich wrote as part of his nomination of his friend to the Georgia Sports Hall of Fame, "In my opinion, George Poschner is perhaps the greatest competitor of all time, both on and off the field. I have never known anyone with more courage on the football or the battle field."

Poschner died in 2004 at the age of eighty-five and was buried with his cane and his red letter jacket from the University of Georgia.

ABOUT THAT FRESHMAN

Charles Louis Trippi grew up in western Pennsylvania the son of a coal miner. At Pittston High School, Trippi was only 160 pounds, but he was noticed by Harold "War Eagle" Ketron. Ketron ran the Coca-Cola bottling plants, but he had played for the Bulldogs in the early 1900s and scouted the area for his alma mater. Back in the 1930s, boosters could offer scholarships, and "War Eagle" Ketron offered one to Trippi.

After completing a year of prep school, Trippi arrived in Athens in 1941 where he played for the Bullpups, UGA's freshman team. That year, the Bullpups went undefeated and Trippi was the star. Trippi joined the Bulldog varsity team and shared the backfield with Frank Sinkwich. Midway through the 1942 season, Coach Butts decided to put Trippi in at halfback and switch Sinkwich to fullback. Trippi gained 1,239 yards of total offense during Sinkwich's Heisman Trophy season. Trippi gained 130 yards in the Rose Bowl win over UCLA, earning him Rose Bowl Most Valuable Player honors.

Charley Trippi. *Georgia Athletic Association.*

World War II interrupted Trippi's college career. Trippi served in the Third Air Force and stayed in football shape playing service football. He missed the 1943 and 1944 seasons and part of the 1945 season serving in the air force. By the time Trippi returned to Georgia midway through the 1945 season, Head Coach Wally Butts had changed the Bulldogs' offense. Butts had switched from the single wing to a T- formation. The new offense gave Trippi the opportunity to throw the ball.

In the 1945 season finale against Georgia Tech, Trippi threw for a then conference record 323 yards against the Yellow Jackets and ran for another 61 yards, which totaled a record 384 yards of total offense. Trippi and the Bulldogs went to the Oil Bowl in Houston, Texas, where he threw a touchdown pass and ran a punt back 68 yards for a score. That punt return is considered by many Bulldog fans to be one of the most spectacular plays in UGA history.

By the time Trippi entered his senior season in 1946, he was known as the "One Man Gang." As a captain of the '46 Bulldogs, he led Georgia to an undefeated season and another SEC Championship. Trippi led the SEC in scoring with 85 points (fourteen touchdowns), rushing for 744 yards and passing for 622 yards. Georgia capped off the 1946 season with a 20–10 win over North Carolina in the Sugar Bowl to complete the Bulldogs' first undefeated season. Trippi won the Maxwell Award and Walter Camp Trophies, but the Heisman Trophy eluded him, going to Army's Glenn Davis—angering Bulldogs supporters and Coach Butts. The Bulldogs were awarded part of the national championship in addition to their second SEC title that year.

The 1946 squad never finished higher than third in the Associated Press rankings with their 11-0 record, but the Williamson System gave the title to the SEC co-champs. Army and Notre Dame split the title that year in the AP poll after a scoreless tie in Yankee Stadium. The four-year record of the 1941 recruiting class was 40-4-1, with two SEC and two national championships.

After graduating, Trippi played two years of baseball before being at the center of a bidding war between the Chicago Cardinals and the New York Yankees of the All-American Football Conference. The Yankees thought that they had him, but Charles Bidwill Sr. inked Trippi to a four-year deal worth $100,000. Trippi's presence completed Bidwill's "Dream Backfield" along with Paul Christman, Pat Harder, Marshall Goldberg and Elmer Angsman. Trippi went on to a brilliant nine-year career in the National Football League (all with the Cardinals), where he won an

NFL championship his rookie year in 1947. His ingenuity was on display in the title game when he wore basketball shoes for better traction. He scored touchdowns on a forty-four-yard run and a seventy-five-yard punt return in the 28–21 win over the Philadelphia Eagles.

In 1968, Trippi was inducted into the Pro Football Hall of Fame, and to this day, he is the only Hall of Famer with 1,000 yards receiving, 1,000 yards passing and 1,000 yards rushing in a career. He was also elected to the College Football Hall of Fame in 1959 and the Georgia Sports Hall of Fame in 1965.

You can also add Trippi's jersey no. 62 to the list of numbers that have been retired in Athens.

A ONE-YEAR WONDER ON THE FLATS

A lot of people wonder if Clint Castleberry could have been one of the greatest of all time. In one year, he certainly left his mark at Georgia Tech.

For the 1942 season, Georgia Tech was thought to be no better than eighth in the twelve-team SEC. Its schedule had Georgia, Alabama, Auburn and Duke. Three of those teams were listed in the preseason top ten, and the Blue Devils had just come off an appearance in the Rose Bowl. Add to that Navy and Notre Dame and Coach William Alexander thought that his young team would be lucky to win five games. But the early focus was on the five-foot, nine-inch 145-pound freshman who had graduated from Boys High just down the street.

After a season-opening win over Auburn, the Yellow Jackets traveled to Notre Dame for their game with the Fighting Irish. Castleberry recovered an Angelo Bertelli fumble and drove for a score, with more to come in the fourth quarter. On what looked like an end-around from the eight-yard line, Castleberry surprised the home team with a touchdown pass good enough for the 13–7 win, garnering him the only freshman spot on the Associated Press SEC Team of the Week. It was Notre Dame's first loss in eleven games. After the win over Chattanooga, Tech was ranked sixth in the country. After a Davidson win, the Williamson Poll ranked Tech third behind Alabama and Georgia, and local sportswriters labeled the young team a "Team of Destiny."

Clint Castleberry…the best there ever was at Tech? *Georgia Tech Athletic Association.*

Next was a nationally televised game with 2-2 Navy. In the second quarter, Castleberry was sent into the game on defense and returned an interception ninety-five yards for a score. His performance on both sides of the ball would give Tech the shutout and praise for his work as related by Richard McMurry in the 1983 *Atlanta Historical Journal*. Bob Considine called him "an embryo All-American if I ever saw one," and a writer for the *New York Herald* had praise for his "speed and shiftiness...[which] combined the best features of a wraith and an antelope." Why, asked a writer for the *Washington Post*, hadn't the eastern press heard of this fine player before the Navy game?

With Alabama, Georgia and Georgia Tech all highly ranked in the polls, it meant the round-robin play in the SEC among them would decide everything. But they would have to do it without Coach Alex. His doctor ordered him to bed for two weeks of rest because of health concerns, and lead assistant Bobby Dodd took over for the games against Kentucky and Alabama. The game against the Crimson Tide was Homecoming for the Jackets, and an announced crowd of thirty-two thousand was at Grant Field for the coming-out party for Clinton Dillard Castleberry Jr.

Off a first-quarter Alabama punt, Castleberry returned it twenty-eight yards to the Tech forty-yard line. On the same drive, he ran for another twenty, caught a pass for thirty-one, ran for another five and was a part of the fake that would eventually set up a Ralph Plaster one-yard touchdown run—the first given up by Alabama all season. Tech held the Tide from scoring on six different occasions, and Castleberry was active all over the field in the win. Fred Russell, of the *Nashville Banner* newspaper, wrote, "I know of only one way to stop Castleberry, and that's to repeal the freshman eligibility rule."

The win the following week by Tech over Florida, combined with the surprising loss of Georgia to Auburn, set the table for the thirty-sixth renewal of the Georgia–Georgia Tech game in Athens. But there were a few concerns, the biggest being the knee of Castleberry that had been injured in the Florida game. Other thoughts were shared by Coach Alex, who told a friend the day before the game:

> *We are in for a bad day, and there's nothing Dodd can do about it. The team is "shot." It showed that in the Florida game. Dodd has done everything a coach can do, but in this day and time, a small frail team with inadequate replacements cannot reach four peaks in one season. We reached a peak for Notre Dame in early October. We reached another for Navy in late October*

and held it a week for Duke. We reached a third for Alabama in mid-November, and exhaustion has set in.

Coach Alex made a point to drive in a car without a radio during the game, and it seems he had the right idea. Castleberry's knee gave way when he was tackled on a second-quarter run, and Tech couldn't match Frank Sinkwich and the Bulldogs on the day of the 34–0 win in Athens. But Alexander did receive a phone call from Dana Bible, the head coach of the University of Texas–Austin, to see if his Jackets would want to play his team on New Year's Day in the Cotton Bowl in Dallas. The final Williamson poll had Tech ranked third, while the AP poll had them fifth.

Castleberry was selected for the all-SEC team with one junior and nine seniors and was named as either a second- or third-team all-American. Voting for the Heisman Trophy was a little different in the early days of the award. Votes were counted both nationally and regionally, with each voter choosing one player nationally and another from his region.

Castleberry finished second to Frank Sinkwich in the Southeast. No freshman had ever done that. Alexander was given national Coach of the Year honors and was allowed to help coach for the bowl game as long as he took it easy and watched his diet.

Castleberry played only a little in the Cotton Bowl. Tech came up short, 14–7, when a last-minute drive was stopped deep in Texas territory. He underwent an operation on his knee in January 1943 before going into service in the U.S. Army Air Corps. On November 6, 1944, a B-26G Marauder nicknamed "Dream Girl" arrived at Roberts Field in Liberia on a ferry mission from Brazil to North Africa. The next morning, the plane was supposed to make it to Dakar, Senegal, with another B-26. The co-pilot was Castleberry, who had made it to the rank of second lieutenant. The pilot and three other crewmen were also on board, but neither plane was heard from ever again. The thought is that the planes collided and fell into the Atlantic Ocean. After a six-day search, a British aircraft found some debris, and that was about all that could be found of either plane. On the twenty-third, Castleberry's status was changed from "missing" to "killed."

His father held out hope until his own death that Clint would appear alive one day somewhere in Africa. He believed that if Clint had survived the crash, he had enough heart to make it through anything. The Tech student body even spearheaded a campaign to create a memorial fund for him, and the end result was a $4,079,100 war bond purchase made in his honor.

Coach Alex. *Georgia Tech Athletic Association.*

In eulogizing Clint Castleberry, Bobby Dodd clearly stated that, had he not left Tech to join the war, he would have been "the greatest player in Tech history" and would surely have been "an all-American for his remaining three years...He was a great boy: gentle and brave, manly yet sweet." Castleberry's no. 19 was retired, the only player in Tech's history to have that honor. Everyone wonders what might have been with Castleberry had wartime not intervened.

Alexander coached at Tech for two more years, going 7-3-0 in 1943 (winning in the Sugar Bowl) and 8-2-0 in 1944 (losing in the Orange Bowl). In 1945, his long illness forced him to retire and turn the head coaching duties over to Dodd. In twenty-five seasons, Alexander finished 134-95-15, and Tech became the first school to play in all four major bowls of the time (Rose, 1929; Orange, 1940 and 1945; Cotton, 1943; and Sugar, 1944). On April 23, 1950, Alex died peacefully in his sleep. Knute Rockne paid Alexander the great compliment when he said that he "gets more out of less than any coach in America."

THE 1950S

ONE BOBBY DODD WAY

In the middle of the 1930 season, William Alexander sent his line coach, Mac Tharpe, to scout the University of North Carolina, which was playing Tennessee in Knoxville. As the story goes, Tharpe's automobile broke down on the way to the game, and by the time he got to Knoxville, the game was over. Tharpe still needed his recon, so he tried to track down Tennessee head coach General Robert Neyland. Neyland sent Tharpe to his quarterback, Robert E. Lee (Bobby) Dodd. When Tharpe returned to campus, he told Coach Alexander that "Dodd's analysis of Carolina is better than any scouting report that I could have made."

Alexander also read about how Dodd turned what could have been a defensive score by Vanderbilt into a huge touchdown for Tennessee in their 1930 win over Vandy. So, with Dodd's college football career barely over, Alexander signed Dodd on as an assistant to his staff on December 28, 1930, for $300 per month. Coach Alexander offered Dodd a $600 bonus if he would report in time for spring football practice.

"That $600 was more money than I had ever seen," Dodd said. "I used about $500 of it paying off debts I had accumulated in Knoxville. And you know, in all the years I was at Georgia Tech, I never had a contract." The all-

American took what he learned from General Neyland—all the ideas about precision, not hitting in practice but rather working on the game itself and making sure his players all studied and graduated (something Dodd always regretted since he never got his degree)—and take the local kid to be a part of his two decades of success on campus.

The 10-1 season and Orange Bowl win set the table for a run in the early 1950s that made Tech the top of the ladder in not only the SEC but nationally as well. The year 1950 was an unspectacular 5-6, but the '51 and '52 years yielded eight different all-Americans and the first twenty-four games in a thirty-three-game unbeaten streak that worked its way into the 1953 season. Dodd and his two assistants, Frank Broyles and Ray Graves, all ended up in the College Football Hall of Fame when their careers were done.

In 1951, guard Ray Beck and defensive tackle Lamar Wheat got those honors for a team that would finish fifth in the final rankings. For 1952, add linebacker George Morris, center Pete Brown, halfback Leon Hardeman, tackle Hal Miller, end Buck Martin and defensive back Bobby Moorhead.

The 1951 team only gave up double-digit points twice (fourteen to both Duke and Baylor in the Orange Bowl), was a co-champ with Tennessee in the SEC and got some national championship consideration in two polls: the Berryman and Boand System. Sophomore halfback Leon Hardeman led the ground attack with local fullback senior George Maloof, and junior Buck Martin was the team's leading scorer.

They actually trailed 14–7 in the Orange Bowl with seven minutes to go, but Darrell Crawford hit Buck Martin with a twenty-two-yard touchdown pass. Three minutes later, Pete Farris intercepted a Larry Isbell pass and returned it to the nine. The Baylor defense wouldn't allow a score, so Dodd sent Pepper Rodgers in to kick the game-winning field goal on fourth down.

1951, 11-0-1, 7-0, SEC/1ˢᵗ (CHAMPIONS), ORANGE BOWL (W)

September 22, 1951, SMU	W, 21–7
September 29, 1951, Florida	W, 27–0
October 6, 1951, Kentucky	W, 13–7
October 13, 1951, LSU	W, 25–7
October 20, 1951, Auburn	W, 27–7
October 27, 1951, Vanderbilt	W, 8–7

The man who replaced Alexander, Robert E. Lee Dodd. *Georgia Tech Athletic Association.*

November 3, 1951, Duke	T, 14–14
November 10, 1951, VMI	W, 34–7
November 17, 1951, Alabama	W, 27–7
November 24, 1951, Davidson	W, 34–7
December 1, 1951, Georgia	W, 48–6
January 1, 1952, Baylor (Orange Bowl)	W, 17–14

1952, 12-0, 6-0, SEC/1ST (CHAMPIONS), SUGAR BOWL (W), CO-NATIONAL CHAMPIONS

Dodd himself referred to the 1952 squad as "the best team I ever coached." Hardeman led the offense in scoring in 1952, while Hardeman, Glenn Turner and Bill Teas each cleared over 650 yards rushing for Dodd in 1952. Martin led the team in receiving, both yards and touchdowns. Morris, the team co-captain, led the team in tackles with 114.

September 20, 1952, The Citadel	W, 54–6
September 27, 1952, Florida	W, 17–14
October 4, 1952, SMU	W, 20–7
October 11, 1952, Tulane	W, 14–0
October 18, 1952, Auburn	W, 33–0
October 25, 1952, Vanderbilt	W, 30–0
November 1, 1952, Duke	W, 28–7
November 8, 1952, Army	W, 45–6
November 15, 1952, Alabama	W, 7–3
November 22, 1952, Florida State	W, 30–0
November 29, 1952, Georgia	W, 23–9
January 1, 1953, Mississippi (Sugar Bowl)	W, 24–7

Tech's appearance in the New Orleans bowl game was part of one of the wildest scrambles in bowl history. The NCAA told its member schools

The all-Americans in 1952. *Georgia Tech Athletic Association.*

not to make any commitments beyond January 2. The Southern and Big
Seven Conferences took positions that kept their member schools from
participating, and everyone thought, with the schools that were left, that
Georgia Tech was heading back to the Orange Bowl again. But after
the win over Army, then Sugar Bowl chair Fred Digby went to Bobby
Dodd and offered him a spot with four games left on the schedule. Dodd
accepted, but the story was denied publicly. As the longtime *New Orleans
Times-Picayune* writer Marty Mulé told the story:

> *Dodd, it seems, grabbed the Sugar because of an offer of 14,000 tickets
> (1,500 more than SEC requirement) for Tech supporters. That story
> was printed and denied by both parties. Before the denial, however, Dodd
> was quoted as saying, "I wanted as many tickets as I could get because
> I don't want Tech fans saying we let them down. We want as many fans
> as can go with us."*

Now, all Tech needed to do was win out and get an opponent. It was thought that Maryland or Oklahoma would go against their conference's view and play, but another option was Mississippi, which started the year with two ties and had gone undefeated since. What people thought was the upset of the year gave Ole Miss its bid: a win over Maryland and a seventh-place ranking to go with its first bowl bid since 1936.

Hardeman and Teas came into the game injured as Tech was a seven-point favorite. Mississippi's QB, Jim "King" Lear, got his team on the board first, but two fumbles and a turnover on downs—two of those plays involving Tech goal-line stands—put the score at 7–7 instead of 14–0, and Tech led 10–7 at the break.

"When we went into the locker room, I remember Coach Dodd sitting on a table, swinging his legs and drinking a Coke," said George Morris, the pride of Vicksburg, Mississippi. "He said, 'Well, boys, it looks like we got 'em on the run.' Our reaction was that Coach Dodd wasn't watching the same game we were."

Another Ole Miss fumble led to a Hardeman score—one that the defense thought was not a score—and a fair catch/not a fumble or a not a fair catch/fumble (depending on whose side you rooted for that day) kept Tech's lead at 17–7. A Pepper Rodgers TD pass in the fourth quarter to Jeff Knox gave the Jackets a comfortable win and an undefeated season. But the written word was less than kind to the officials trying to leave town under cover of darkness. Mulé relayed again that surely a conspiracy was afoot.

"Three of the four officials who worked in the Sugar Bowl live in Georgia," *Times-Picayune* sports editor Bill Keefe couldn't resist noting. "Two are from Atlanta. Mississippi Governor Hugh White sent letters to George Gardner, president of the SEC Officials Association, and to Bernie Moore, SEC commissioner, saying he had witnessed the worst officiating I have ever seen."

A Rebel fan spotted Ole Miss president Dr. John Davis Williams walking from the stadium and said, "Well, Doc, I see you've still got your watch and chain, so maybe we're lucky."

The Berryman, International News Service and Massey Ratings and Poling System all voted Tech national title-holders for the year. The 1953 Sugar Bowl was also the first broadcast nationally on ABC. It took some doing, and it was a race to the finish, but a deal was struck. The national head of the March of Dimes encouraged AT&T to extend its coaxial cable construction to New Orleans as its donation to the charity since it was the major benefactor.

The team's thirty-one-game unbeaten streak came to an end after a 4-0-1 start in 1954 with a 27–14 loss at Notre Dame in South Bend. But Dodd's Jackets spent the next three seasons going 27-5-1, placing runner-up in the SEC twice and winning the Cotton, Sugar and Gator Bowl games. For one of those three bowl games, the 1956 Sugar Bowl, there was some doubt that it actually would be played.

THE BIGGEST WIN, OFF THE FIELD

Tech (7-1-1) was set to play 7-2 Pittsburgh, but the mere presence of running back Bobby Grier in the Panther backfield caused controversy and debate as to why the game should even be played. Grier was black, and then Georgia governor Marvin Griffin was opposed to integration. Pete Thamel wrote about the game and Grier's place in history for a fiftieth-anniversary piece on that Sugar Bowl in the *New York Times*:

> *"The South stands at Armageddon," Griffin said in a telegram to Georgia's Board of Regents, detailing his request that teams in the state's university system not participate in events in which races were mixed on the field or in the stands.*
>
> *"The battle is joined. We cannot make the slightest concession to the enemy in this dark and lamentable hour of struggle.*
>
> *One break in the dike and the relentless seas will push in and destroy us. We are in this fight 100 percent."*

The day before Griffin made his stance, Rosa Parks refused to yield her seat on a Montgomery, Alabama bus. Georgia Tech's students burned Griffin in effigy in front of the state capitol and marched on the governor's mansion. Pittsburgh's entire group of supporters—in and out of the administration—would only be a part of the Sugar Bowl if Grier was able to play and those attending the game were not going to be placed in segregated seating at Tulane Stadium. The team stayed on the Tulane campus because of segregation in New Orleans, but Grier broke a barrier by attending part of the week's celebrations at the St. Charles Hotel.

Tech won the game, 7–0, and finished ranked seventh in the country. The decisive play was one against Grier while he was playing defense: a pass interference call that led to the only touchdown of the game. But win or lose, Grier's impact remains to this day for playing a game in the Deep South when a lot of individuals wanted no such thing. "I learned that things were going to change and things were a hanging'," he told Thamel. "It showed that sports has a way to change a whole lot of things."

Change would be very slow in some circles. In 1957, *Atlanta Journal* columnist Jim Minter took the unprecedented step of using his pages to openly go against Governor Griffin when a state bill proposed a ban of integrated athletics and other social activities. Griffin reinforced his personal stance, saying that the bill he endorsed would make sure that "Negroes and white folks playing any type of sport together" shouldn't happen.

Bowl games and other successes aside, Bobby Dodd became more and more disenchanted with life in the SEC. He saw the landscape changing, much as Thornwell Jacobs had up Peachtree Road thirty years earlier from his post at Oglethorpe University.

In an interview with *Sports Illustrated* as he prepared for the 1957 game with Auburn University and Shug Jordan, Dodd talked with Don Parker about seeing the recruiting aspect of college football becoming more and more prevalent, with less of a focus on academics and pursuing young men honestly:

> *Recruiting has gotten too far out of hand. Illegal recruiting…I mean the kind where a coach will go out and offer a kid the world with a fence around it—it's going to ruin football. It's bad enough now, and if it gets any worse I'll have to stand up and say, "Let's get rid of intercollegiate football. Let's play on an intramural basis. But let's play it honest."*
>
> *Down here in the Southeastern Conference we have a recruiting deadline. We can't sign a boy to a scholarship until midnight, December 7. You know what some of the coaches do to get a kid? They'll take them off to the mountains on a fishing trip and hide them out for a few days before the deadline. Then they sign them right at midnight and the fishing trip is over. It almost amounts to kidnapping. We've never done that here at Tech. In fact, it has been rare that we've signed anybody right on the deadline. I think I signed one boy at midnight this year and that was because he asked me to. He said it would save him from being pestered all night by other schools.*

It was the first step in a process by Dodd that would eventually see the team take a drastic step for the time but one that is quite commonplace today.

THE DROUGHT BREAKER

Theron Sapp's career numbers won't ever come close to those of names like Walker, Sinkwich, Moreno, Trippi, Davis or, frankly, anyone else at the position of tailback. He became a University of Georgia legend not for his career but rather for one play that restored Georgia pride and broke a long losing streak.

Sapp has his place among Bulldog greats for the frigid afternoon of November 30, 1957, at Grant Field in Atlanta. The Bulldogs were about to end another losing season, Georgia's third in a row. Wally Butts's team went through an uncharacteristic stretch of sub-.500 seasons throughout the decade, going 3-8 in 1953, 4-6 in 1955 and 3-6-1 in 1956, and it was taking on archrival Georgia Tech at 2-7 in 1957. Tech had dominated the series recently—1948 was the last time the Bulldogs had defeated the team. Georgia hadn't even scored a touchdown on Tech since 1953.

Sapp was Georgia's best back, leading the Bulldogs in rushing in 1957 and again in 1958. Both teams were finding it difficult to move the ball in the below-freezing temperatures, but the Bulldogs got a big break late in the third quarter recovering a Tech fumble at midfield. Georgia drove the ball down the field behind Sapp, who carried the ball eight times on the drive as the Bulldogs marched to the Yellow Jackets' one-yard line.

On fourth down and goal, Sapp took the handoff from quarterback Charley Britt, started right and then found a gap and fell into the end zone for the touchdown. Georgia defeated Tech, 7–0. Bulldog pride was restored in the short term, and Sapp was known as the "Drought Breaker" for the rest of his life. It even inspired an Atlanta lawyer named Harold M. Walker to pen a poem titled "The Man Who Broke the Drought":

> *You can rave about your Sinkwich*
> *And Trippi's praises sing.*
> *While talk about the "Bowl Days"*
> *Still makes the welkin ring.*

But to all Bulldog supporters
In every precinct in the South
I propose a hearty toast
To the man who broke the drought.

Rise up you loyal Georgians
From Tybee Light to Rabun Gap
Here's to the Macon Mauler
The mighty Theron Sapp

I have seen some lovely paintings
In galleries of art,
Gorgeous sunsets on the water
Which stirred the inner heart.

But of all the wonderous visions
Ever seen by eyes of mine,
I'll take old number forty
Crashing through that Jacket line.

And so down through the ages
Whenever Bulldogs meet,
Whether in the peaceful countryside
Or on a crowded street.

The word will still be carried
By every loyal mouth—
Let's stand and drink another toast
To the man who broke the drought!

In 1958, Georgia was going through a 3-6 season when they defeated Tech again, 16–3, in Theron Sapp's final college game. Sapp only scored six touchdowns in his Georgia career, but months later, at the annual G-Day game that ends spring practice, he became the third Bulldog to have his jersey number retired. No. 40 would forever belong to the man who broke the drought.

Francis Tarkenton

After his family moved to Athens from the Washington, D.C., area in 1952, Fran Tarkenton became a tremendous athlete at Athens High School. During his career with the Athens High Gladiators, Tarkenton earned all-state honors in basketball, baseball and football. As the quarterback, Tarkenton led Athens High to a 41–20 victory over Mercer graduate Wright Bazemore, who was coaching state power Valdosta for the 1955 state championship.

Tarkenton enrolled at the University of Georgia in 1957 and led the Bullpups to an undefeated season. The year 1958 was supposed to be a red-shirt year for Tarkenton, but in Georgia's season opener, hosting the Texas Longhorns, they were trailing, 7–0, midway through the third quarter. Without telling the Georgia coaching staff, Tarkenton inserted himself into the lineup, replacing starting quarterback Tommy Lewis.

"They wanted to red-shirt me and I didn't want to because I thought I could help the team," Tarkenton told the *Athens Banner Herald* years later. "So I just bolted onto the field. I put myself in."

Beginning from Georgia's own five-yard line, Tarkenton led a twenty-one-play, ninety-five-yard drive ending in a three-yard touchdown pass to Jimmy Vickers. When Georgia head coach Wally Butts sent the kicking unit in for the extra point, Tarkenton waved them off, taking it upon himself to go for two. The sophomore completed a pass to Aaron Box for the two-point conversion. It was that kind of risk-taking that defined Fran Tarkenton.

The next season, Tarkenton took another risk that paid off by drawing up a play on the turf against Auburn in Athens. Trailing the Tigers, 13–7, late in the game, Coach Butts sent in a play and Tarkenton ignored it. "I knew we needed something different," Tarkenton said when asked about it years later. "I told the left end Bill Herron, who was in tight, to really go ahead and make a block. I told him 'count to a thousand-four and then run to the left corner of the end zone.'"

Herron followed Tarkenton's instructions and made the catch to defeat Auburn, 14–13, and win the 1959 SEC Championship. Georgia met the Missouri Tigers in the Orange Bowl. Tarkenton threw two touchdowns to Bill McKenney and Aaron Box as the Bulldogs shut out the Tigers, 14–0. He finished the day going only 9 for 16 for 120 yards and the two scores in front of a crowd of 75,260. Tigers head coach

Fran Tarkenton would scramble at an early age. *Georgia Athletic Association.*

Dan Devine had won his last three in a row to get his team to Miami with a 6-4 record as Big Eight Conference champs. They finished the year ranked eighteenth in the Associated Press poll and nineteenth in the UPI poll—even with the loss.

As a senior in 1960, Tarkenton led the SEC in total offense with 1,274 yards and passing yards with 1,189, earning all-American honors. However, the Bulldogs finished a disappointing 6-4 in Wally Butts' last season as coach. Tarkenton went on to a Hall of Fame career in the NFL with the New York Giants and the Minnesota Vikings, leading the Vikings to three Super Bowls, and he can be seen on television these days as an analyst on political and financial programs.

BOBBY AND HIS BOYS

Before Johnny Griffith had a major head coaching job in the 1960s, he ended up in Coffee County, in southeast Georgia, getting his feet wet at South Georgia College from 1950 to 1954. He played there in the 1940s and acted as an assistant coach in 1949. In four years, he ended up with a 32-6 record and took his team to four bowl appearances.

But two years after Griffith left, a young twenty-five-year-old Bobby Bowden took over the Tigers. Bowden actually was athletic director, baseball coach, football coach and basketball coach before exclusively sticking to football—learning his lesson about basketball going 1-13 in 1955. His salary was $4,200 with a wife and three kids. He lived in the old army barracks of the Sixty-third Flight Training Detachment, which was active during World War II, at a cost of $25 per month. He drove the school bus, the "Old Blue Goose," for the team as it went from game to game. Most of his players were Korean War veterans who were older than their coach—they still wore leather helmets and ran out of the T-formation.

He debated growing his hair out, cutting it short and changing his name to "Robert" Bowden to look or sound older, but the Tigers won three Georgia junior college championships in Bowden's four seasons and he was named the state's Junior College Coach of the Year in 1955 and 1957.

Terry Bowden was actually born in Douglas, and he recalled his family's early years in a Father's Day column for Yahoo!Sports in 2008:

> *During those days, my family lived in a dorm on campus and as a toddler I often wandered across the grounds among the students. There is a story that I have heard told and retold countless times of how the players would constantly feed me candy and co-colas when I would wander out onto the campus. One day my mother pinned a sign on the back of my diaper that said "do not feed" and sent me out to play in the school courtyard. A couple of hours later I came back home with the sign turned over and inscribed with the words, "well fed."*

In 1956, Bobby's wife, Ann, won the Mrs. South Georgia contest while working part time as a substitute teacher and in a Sears mail-order store. Bobby worked as a lifeguard and in a tobacco warehouse to help make ends meet.

After Bowden's 1958 season, the school president told Bowden that the school had to stop the football program because of a lack of money. He was asked to stay on as athletic director and baseball coach, but he told them no and went back to Howard College in Birmingham with a dozen of his Tigers in tow.

One More for the Decade

In the central Georgia town of Milledgeville, Georgia Military College (GMC) was another successful junior college program under the guidance of Llewellyn "Lew" Cordell. In his senior year at the University of Georgia, Cordell signed a contract with the Chicago Bears but changed his mind and headed for GMC to coach. After only one year, Cordell became head coach and stayed until the program stopped operations in 1958.

He finished with a record of 118-36-7 and ended up with twelve state and southeastern regional junior college championships. Cordell was inducted into the Georgia State Hall of Fame in 1982, and three years later, GMC renamed the field house the Cordell Events Center.

GMC's football program was reinstated in 1991 and experienced another renaissance of its own.

THE 1960S

THE BEST TEAM NO ONE KNOWS ABOUT

In 1960, the Albany State College squad went down in history as a team that went through an entire season without being scored on and thus were unbeaten. While records on Obie O'Neal Jr.'s team are scarce, one of its wins was against Savannah State, recorded in the November version of the *Tiger's Roar* newsletter:

> *Albany's Mel Bostic and Ed Nelson provided a two-man offensive show for the unbeaten and unscored upon Albany State College as the ASC Rams upended SSC's Tigers 19–0. Albany co-Captain Bostic returned Ben Edwards' game opening kick-off 80 yards for the first score and received a 31-yard pass from quarterback Art Gamble for another. Bostic, a 205 pounder who is used at any backfield position and at end, sped through the entire Tiger defense for the first touchdown.*
>
> *A 22-yard field goal in the third quarter was nullified by an offside penalty. Nelson, a reserve Ram fullback and kicking specialist, fell on the ball in the end zone in the fourth period after Tiger John Strong made an attempt for Nelson's kickoff. Nelson also kicked the extra point for the final score.*

End Fred Carter and Linebacker Robert Leonard were outstanding defensively for the Tigers.

O'Neal coached both football and basketball on campus. Records vary on the actual years. One source has him coaching football from 1951 to 1962 while another has him coaching from 1961 to 1967 with a career mark of 79-57-10. He was also head coach of the men's basketball team from 1951 to 1958. He and his remarkable team have their place in the Albany Sports Hall of Fame for their efforts long ago.

THE END OF AN ERA AND THE BEGINNING OF A FEW MORE

The year 1960 would be the last football season coaching in Athens for James Wallace Butts Jr. By the time the "Little Round Man" wrapped up his career, he finished 140-86-9 with four SEC titles and appearances in eight bowl games. Butts was SEC Coach of the Year twice and garnered National Coach of the Year in 1946. He then stayed on as athletic director, but one event marked his last few seasons on campus.

On March 22, 1963, the *Saturday Evening Post* published a story entitled "The Story of a College Football Fix" claiming that Butts and Alabama head football coach Bear Bryant "fixed" the 1962 Georgia-Alabama game. The Tide won the game, 35–0, and both coaches sued the *Post* for libel to the tune of $10 million each.

A gentleman named George Burnett claimed that he accidentally overheard, and took notes on, a September telephone conversation between Butts and Bryant. Butts allegedly gave Bryant information on plays that Georgia was going to use in the game. Four months later, Burnett started talking to people, including then Georgia coach Johnny Griffith and the *Post*. Frank Graham Jr. was assigned by the *Post* to work the story, and Furman Bisher, then editor of the *Atlanta Journal*, was supposed to advise him. Graham never saw Burnett's notes and never talked to Butts or Bryant.

Both Butts and Bryant testified at the trial and denied any kind of conversation regarding what Graham claimed to be true. Football players testified that it would be hard to "fix" a game without their involvement in any kind of plot to do so, and witnesses called in Butts's defense denied saying what was attributed to them in the article.

Butts's attorneys, William Schroder and Allen Lockerman, gave his defense. Schroder was a Notre Dame football player and received his law degree from UGA, while Lockerman was one of the Federal Bureau of Investigation (FBI) agents responsible for gunning down John Dillinger. In Schroder's close, as reported by Robert H. Boyle in *Sports Illustrated*, he told the jury, "Someday, as must happen to each of us, Wallace Butts will pass on where neither the *Post* nor anyone else can then bother him. Unless I miss my guess, they will put him in a red coffin with a black lid with a football in his hands, and his epitaph will read, 'Glory, glory to Old Georgia.'"

They won the case, and Butts was awarded more than $3 million, the largest plaintiff award for a libel suit at the time. The award was lowered to a little under $500,000, but Butts's reputation still took a major hit. The case made it all the way to the United States Supreme Court, where it was combined with another case to determine whether or not the malice standard applied to freedom of the press in June 1967.

Coach Bryant eventually settled out of court as well. The verdict was even seen in some circles as the beginning of the end of the *Post*. One of the first things Butts did after returning home to Athens when the verdict came down was simply to go to the grocery store and pick up some stale bread to feed the birds in his backyard.

Pressure was felt by Griffith and university President O.C. Aderhold, who testified against Butts at the trial. Aderhold was even treated poorly at a local country club afterward. One Bulldog alum even told *Sports Illustrated* that they were "dusting off a chair for a president emeritus."

Butts eventually resigned as athletic director, and his Bulldog era came to a close. He died of a heart attack after coming home from a walk in 1973 at the age of sixty-eight, and he is buried at Oconee Hill Cemetery. The "Little Round Man" was elected to the Georgia Sports Hall of Fame in 1966 and to the College Football Hall of Fame in 1997.

THE SEC WOULD LOSE ONE

The shocking decision started with the Jackets game at Legion Field in 1961. Darwin Holt hit Georgia Tech's Chick Graning during a punt return, and the aftereffects were a broken jaw and a concussion—without a penalty being called. The Atlanta papers showed a picture of Graning in a hospital bed the following week, accused Holt of doing what he did on purpose and pointed the finger at Bear Bryant. Graning would never play football again. Dodd sent a letter to Bryant asking that he suspend Holt after he watched game film and saw that the injury looked intentional. Bryant did not suspend Holt.

The other issue had to do with what was called the "140 Rule." Schools, much like modern-day practices, would overrecruit their numbers for the football team. But in the 1960s, summer practice was used for thinning the herd, and if a coach wasn't interested in a player any longer, he would get cut. That would keep all the other schools from getting a player they might have had interest in during their initial recruitment. Dodd wanted the SEC administration to punish schools that participated in that practice. They didn't.

Before an SEC meeting in January 1964, Tech president Edwin Harrison announced that the school was leaving the conference rather than issue an ultimatum about the 140 Rule (either the rule would be rescinded or Tech would leave). The *Spartanburg Herald-Journal* reported from the meeting where Harrison said, "Our action neither indicates nor implies criticisms of other institutions or of the conference, but rather acknowledges a uniqueness of our situation."

Coach Dodd added:

> *We would have stayed in if this rule had been lifted. A careful survey of prospective student-athletes and a well-planned program of tutoring for all that needed it after their arrival has cut our losses of scholarship-athletes to a figure much below that of most conference schools. This has resulted in limiting our recruiting program to the extent that we feel we cannot comply with the rule and continue to field a respectable team. This is not fair to our school, our alumni, our players, or anyone connected with the program.*

The conference stayed at eleven teams for the 1964 season, and no scheduled games that Tech had with SEC schools were affected. President Harrison hugged SEC commissioner Bernie Moore at a press conference, told him that he still loved him and admitted that entering another conference would be difficult since "no other technological school in the country has the same problems we have trying to play football."

The Ramblin' Wreck, circa 1969.
Georgia Tech Athletic Association.

Tech stayed as an independent like Notre Dame and Penn State for the last four years Dodd coached at Tech. Dodd told *Sports Illustrated*'s Dan Jenkins leading up to the yearly contest with Georgia that the 1966 team (his last) was his favorite: "It doesn't have the ability of the 1951 or 1952 teams, or even the 1956 team. Not as many athletes. But it has something special—the big-play quality. We've sure made some big plays when they counted."

Jenkins described the team as "a grand mixture of players from 11 different states, of a host of married guys, of baseball players, of preachers, of a lot of fullbacks playing defense, of a golf champion for a place-kicker, a basketball forward filling in presently at quarterback—and all of them light, quick and prideful."

The team went into the game ranked fifth in the country at 9-0 but lost in Athens and in the Orange Bowl to Florida for a final ranking of eighth in both the AP and UPI polls. Lenny Snow, the preacher Jenkins mentioned above, rather preferred speaking at Fellowship of Christian Athletes gatherings than to the press during his time on campus. But his actions on the field added his name to the list of all-Americans on campus.

In 1967, Dodd had Bud Carson take over after his retirement as head coach. He stayed on as athletic director.

AS BOBBY WAS LEAVING,
VINCE WAS GETTING WARMED UP

On November 22, 1963, the same day President John F. Kennedy was assassinated, the University of Georgia hired Joel Eaves as the new athletic director. His first job was to replace Johnny Griffith, who had resigned after three seasons—none of them over .500, 10-16-4 overall and seasons during which Georgia Tech had beaten them each time. Completely unacceptable.

Eaves came to Athens after a successful turn as Auburn's head men's basketball coach. Eaves knew thirty-one-year-old Vince Dooley from his time on campus as a football player and, later, an assistant under Shug Jordan. Jordan told the Associated Press after Dooley was hired, "He will be a great head coach. He has a keen mind and is a great competitor with a tremendous desire to excel."

"There was great turmoil here. But I didn't care," Dooley said in an interview with the *Athens Banner Herald* newspaper later in life. "I came in and went to work and put together a good staff. We all were very close to each other and stayed close and had to establish credibility, and the way you establish credibility is to win football games."

The 1964 season started roughly with a 31–3 loss to eventual national champ Alabama. But Georgia finished the 1964 regular season 6-4, finishing second in the SEC, beating Florida and Georgia Tech and receiving an invitation to the Sun Bowl in El Paso, Texas, where the Bulldogs defeated the Texas Tech Red Raiders, 7–0.

Georgia opened 1965 against Alabama at Sanford Stadium and got a program-establishing win over the Crimson Tide thanks to a little trickery. With just over two minutes left in the game and the Bulldogs down, 17–10, quarterback Kirby Moore completed a pass to Pat Hodgson, who lateraled to halfback Bob Taylor. Taylor went seventy-three yards for the tying score.

Sports Illustrated reported in its September 27 edition that Taylor "moved so fast that no official was able to detect what a sequence camera later showed—Hodgson's knee on the ground while he had possession of the ball. The play should have been dead on the 35. Instead, Taylor raced untouched down the sideline for the touchdown."

Dooley went for two. Moore and Hodgson hooked up again, and Georgia had the 18–17 upset. Dooley was quoted in the same *SI* article referring to the flea-flicker play: "Four years ago [Georgia] Tech used it on us when I was at Auburn, and I thank them very much. We practiced it for two weeks, but I thought it would be 1980 before I'd have the nerve to call it in a game."

Georgia closed the decade of the 1960s with two SEC Championships, the first in 1966. Surprisingly, the run to the title had to go through the Florida Gator and eventual Heisman Trophy winner Steve Spurrier. The Gators were undefeated at 7-0 and ranked seventh in the country, but Vince Dooley had a game plan. His defense, led by sophomore standout Bill Stanfill, blitzed all day and hit Spurrier as hard as it could as often as it could. The Georgia defense picked off Spurrier for a 17–10 lead and followed that up with a field goal and another rushing TD with six seconds left for a 27–10 upset by the unranked Bulldogs. UGA shared the SEC title with Alabama at season's end.

"Steve didn't like you to get close or touch him," Stanfill said after the game. "He'd get up complaining, 'Late hit, late hit!' I said, 'Excuse me, Stevie, I didn't mean to step on your skirt.' Even if he released the ball, his butt was going on the ground. And he didn't like it either. We pounded him. Not only me, but the whole team."

Georgia fans mocked Spurrier in a poem written by Harold Walker:

THE GREATEST OF ALL

Each bowl was there with its special courier,
For a post-game chat with Mr. Spurrier;
But how can you connect with wingback Trapp,
While spending the afternoon in Stanfill's lap?
The Cairo Catamount left the Gators a wreck,
To them he was one large pain-in-the-neck

Stanfill was one of the standouts of Vince Dooley's first recruiting class. In his 1967 junior season, he again earned all-SEC honors, leading the Bulldogs to the Liberty Bowl. He earned all-American honors as a senior, was named SEC Lineman of the Year and was awarded the Outland Trophy as the country's best interior lineman.

The year 1968 ended for the Bulldogs with an SEC Championship and a trip to New Orleans to represent the league in the Sugar Bowl. Though the Bulldogs lost to Arkansas in the Sugar Bowl, Stanfill's record in the red and black was 25-6-2, including three trips to bowl games and a pair of SEC titles.

Dooley said of Stanfill, "He was everything you'd want in a defensive tackle. He combined speed, size, range, quickness and competitiveness to make him one of the greatest linemen to ever play the game." Stanfill was inducted into the College Football Hall of Fame in 1998 and was a key member of the Dolphins' famed "No Name" defense and two Super Bowl championship teams—including the 1972 team that went 17-0, the only undefeated team in NFL history.

Two other names are readily associated with that 1968 team: William Porter "Billy" Payne and Jake Scott. Payne was the local kid (the son of Porter Otis Payne, captain of the 1949 Bulldog football team), student body vice-president, vice-president of the campus chapter of the Fellowship of Christian Athletes, winner of the distinguished service award from the business school and recipient of an honorary doctor of laws. On the field, he started out as a tight end. But before the 1968 season, Coach Dooley asked him to switch over to defensive end since the team was thin at the position. Payne did, received all-SEC honors at end and helped lead the team to the Sugar Bowl.

"I said many times that I've seen some individual specialists at different skills, but I've never seen a better 60-minute man," Dooley said to Loran Smith once for his statewide newspaper column. "If there's one guy you want in the game playing the whole time—offense, defense and kicking—it would be Billy Payne."

Payne had a side few knew about off the field. Billy created a poet persona, "Lamar" (his wife's maiden name), and posted verses in the locker room as the team neared the end of spring practice one year. Each day got a new verse. "They couldn't catch me," he told Loran, "because I might go into the locker room at midnight or 3:00 a.m." He didn't remember any of the poems themselves, but he did recall the tagline: "Oh the coaches are sad, but gee, I'm glad." There's also talk that someone wrote motivational words on the chalkboards during the Sugar Bowl run. Those are also linked to Payne but are unproven to this day.

"My daddy always said, 'Never was a horse that couldn't be rode or a rider that couldn't be throwed,'" Payne said in a 1990 *Sports Illustrated* article. "He would say, 'Billy, if you're not smarter than a lot of people or a better athlete than somebody, you can always outwork 'em.'" Payne has been given four honorary doctorates from four southern schools for his work. He was inducted into the Georgia Sports Hall of Fame. He's been named "Georgian of the Year" by multiple groups, and he is also a recipient of the Theodore Roosevelt Award—the highest honor given by the NCAA.

Payne is always thankful to the University of Georgia for three things: meeting his wife, Martha, at UGA; meeting fellow students during his time there with whom he is still friends; and playing college football like his father did before him.

Jake Scott would be, quoting Winston Churchill, a riddle wrapped in an enigma. The native of Greenville, South Carolina, was an all-SEC and all-American safety and kick returner, but he was known just as much for his exploits and opinions as for his play on the field. He drove over the top of an unfinished Stegeman Coliseum on an old BSA motorcycle but was called by Vince Dooley the best overall athlete Dooley had ever coached. Scott had a great deal of fondness for the 1968 team, noted in an interview with the *Atlanta Journal-Constitution*'s Chip Towers held before Scott's 2011 induction in the College Football Hall of Fame:

> *We had a great football team; we really did. Nobody could block [Bill] Stanfill and we had some great players and some great guys. That's why I thought we should've tried for the national championship. We could play with anybody at the time, except maybe Houston. They had like six No. 1 draft choices.*
>
> *We should have won the Tennessee game. We messed up in that one. We should have lost the Houston game, so things balanced out I guess. You can't worry about it.*

A rift between Dooley and Scott caused him to leave after the season, though. As the story goes, a lot of the players thought that they were in a position to choose which bowl game they could play. Ranked in the top four in the country at the time, they wanted to play Kansas in the Orange Bowl since the top two teams were squaring off in the Rose Bowl. Dooley and the Dogs went elsewhere for the postseason, even as the players thought that they had a chance to have a stake in the national title chase. Scott continued with Towers: "We all wanted the Orange Bowl. We were scheduled to play Kansas in the Orange Bowl. I could be wrong; that's been a million years ago. But I think that's what it was. So everybody on our team was really upset because we felt like, if you've got a chance to go for the ring, go for the ring. You know, what the hell!"

Scott left to play a year of offense for the British Columbia Lions in the Canadian Football League for a year before returning to the NFL and the Miami Dolphins to be another part of that "No Name" defense of the early 1970s with that guy no one could block in college.

Jake Scott. *Georgia Athletic Association.*

THE SOUNDTRACK OF OUR YOUTH

The 1966 championship season was the first of play-by-play for Larry Munson at the University of Georgia. Munson and Milo Hamilton were supposed to be the new broadcast duo for the Atlanta Braves. Munson saw another opportunity for his talents ninety minutes up the road from Atlanta at Fulton County Stadium.

Munson told Dan Magill in 2007 in an article published by the *Athens Banner Herald*, "Early in 1966 I read that Ed Thilenius [Georgia announcer before Munson] had given up his job doing the Georgia football games. So I immediately phone [Joel] Eaves [Georgia athletic director], whom I had known when he was Auburn's basketball coach. His teams played Vandy twice a year. He gave me the job."

Twelve years earlier, Al Ciraldo started his thirty-eight-year run on the rival sideline. He called 416 football and 1,030 basketball games during his tenure there from 1954 to 2002. He stepped away from the play-by-play position after the 1992 season, but he still hosted the pre- and postgame shows. Monsignor Noel Burtenshaw interviewed Ciraldo for the *Georgia Bulletin* in 1979 and asked Tech's voice what he thought about his years behind the microphone—the golden years for Tech, in the 1950s and 1960s. "Bobby Dodd was a legend," said Al with admiration. "He was like Rockne. He also had the love of his players. Players today are faster, better and quicker, because of better diet and better training methods. But coaching under Dodd was magnificent."

Where Munson wasn't accepted as the hometown voice until later, Ciraldo's "toe meets leather" signaled the start of Georgia Tech football games where he would alert the listener to a barnburner by identifying them as "brother and sister" and asking them to hold on. Quarterbacks were always "on the bark," and runs along the sideline involved the "chalk stripes." He graduated from the University of Florida with a degree in radio broadcasting in 1948 and came to Atlanta in 1949.

Before he retired, Ciraldo was elected to the National Sportscaster Hall of Fame, the Georgia Tech Hall of Fame and the Broadcaster's Hall of Fame; was presented Georgia Tech's coveted "T" Award for outstanding service to the Tech community; and had the press box at Bobby Dodd Stadium at Grant Field named in his honor.

Ciraldo had the pleasure of having President Jimmy Carter call the 1977 Georgia Tech–Navy game with him for seven minutes of airtime, and he thought that Eddie Lee Ivery was one of the most talented backs the campus ever saw. "It has always been like this," Ciraldo told the monsignor, "once the game starts, I want those folks out there involved. High school or college, small game or big game, I want them with me."

His longtime color commentator was Tech's starting quarterback from 1965 to 1968, Kim King. He was always introduced as "the young left-hander from Atlanta's own Brown High School."

When Ciraldo passed in 1997, the signal-caller told us all what we already knew: "I've lost a good friend, Georgia Tech lost a good friend, and college football has lost a good friend. He was a throwback to the old days, in terms of virtues and values. He was a man of great loyalty and honesty and integrity. We talk about those virtues in this day and age, but rarely see them."

THE 1970S

INTEGRATION ON BOTH CAMPUSES

In the fall of 1972, Georgia was among the last of three SEC schools (Ole Miss and LSU were the other two) to play black players on their football teams, even though UGA had integrated its track team four years before when Harry Sims and James Hurley were part of the Bulldogs 1968 team.

Hurley played on the JV football squad but never played varsity. John King followed Hurley and became the first African American to actually receive a scholarship for the fall of 1969, but just before the season, he transferred to Minnesota. Then coach Vince Dooley brought in a class that included Horace King, Chuck Kinnebrew, Clarence Pope, Larry West and Richard Appleby in December 1970.

The coaching staff admitted that they had tried in the past to integrate. "It's not that black athletes haven't been approached before," said freshman coach John Donaldson, as reported by Patrick Garbin in his About Them Dawgs! Blog. "They have, but most of them couldn't make the team for academic reasons."

Garbin also found that athletics director Joel Eaves said at the time, "I think [UGA was] just cautious. We were just not sure how it would work out." Eaves added that the athletic department had been specifically cautious about "the mixing and the fact that we're in a section that was slow in integrating."

So, when it comes to UGA's first African American signal-caller, the answer is twofold. Tony Flanagan QB'ed the varsity in 1976, but Troup's Mike Hart was there a year before. Hart was behind Matt Robinson and Ray Goff on the depth chart, but he ended up with his own set of ups and downs as a member of the Bullpups. Hart left school but returned for the Tech JV game and was part of the logjam of the '76 position.

But he never did take a snap on the varsity.

Eddie McAshan

In 1970, Eddie McAshan broke into the starting lineup as quarterback at Georgia Tech as a sophomore and got write-ups in *Jet* and *Ebony* magazines as the first African American quarterback to start for a major southeastern United States university. He led the Yellow Jackets to a win in the Sun Bowl and top-fifteen and top-twenty placements in the two major polls. But by his senior year, regrettably, McAshan would be known more for activity off the field than on, and it took almost two decades to heal the wounds created. It all started over tickets.

Eddie wanted to see if he could get extra tickets for his family to the 1972 Georgia game. The university told him no. McAshan skipped a practice, and then coach Bill Fulcher suspended him from the Georgia game. Tech lost the Georgia game, and Fulcher added the Liberty Bowl game to the suspension.

Lines were drawn as the local black community sided with McAshan and Georgia Tech sided with Fulcher. There was talk of a boycott of the Liberty Bowl, and his black teammates, fearing the loss of their scholarships, even crossed an NAACP picket line outside the Liberty Bowl but wore black armbands in support. Tech won, 31–30, over Iowa State, but McAshan sat outside the stadium in a white stretch limousine with Jesse Jackson. Jackson called him the "Jackie Robinson of Southern college football." There had been death threats on McAshan's life, and there was even the thought that Tech would not play in the game because of it.

But McAshan and the university tried to heal the gap. He graduated seven years later from the school and, along with four of his teammates, had started a scholarship in his name by the late 1990s. "The net result is to get Eddie and Georgia Tech back together. That's the intent," McAshan's teammate, Karl Barnes, told the *Seattle Post-Intelligencer* before the 2000 Florida Citrus Bowl. "This is to lay to rest the whole issue of Eddie McAshan and Georgia Tech."

What people failed to remember for the longest time was that the name of Eddie McAshan was on seventeen different lines of the Yellow Jackets history book before he was through on campus. And his relationship with the school started to heal in time; he was an example for a quarterback who was chasing his records almost two decades later.

Coming Home

After Bobby Dodd's retirement, defensive coordinator Bud Carson was elevated to fill the head coaching position. Carson was succeeded by Bill Fulcher after only one season over .500 in his five. Fulcher was in charge for two years before quitting, and then someone who played for Dodd worked his way from UCLA and Lawrence, Kansas—the guy who kicked the game-winning field goal in the 1951 Orange Bowl and threw a touchdown in the 1952 Sugar Bowl: Franklin C. "Pepper" Rodgers.

Rodgers was "looking to bring the sting back" in the program, thought his old coach and now boss Bobby Dodd. And Rodgers's personality was something that the alumni and fan bases had to get used to upon his arrival. His hair was permed, and he rode to work on a motorcycle. Rodgers even once said that he didn't take himself too seriously even if he took his job seriously. He rubbed the old supporters the wrong way almost immediately, and there was a yearly wonder if he would stay employed. He barely had the team over .500 in his five years on campus, but his lead tailback in 1978 made sure that a crowd just short of twenty thousand in Colorado Springs, Colorado, would witness a record-breaking performance.

Eddie Lee Ivery, the pride of Thomson, Georgia, needed 56 yards to become the first Yellow Jackets running back in modern-day history to clear 1,000 yards in a season. A very ill Ivery ran for 356 yards and three touchdowns in a 42–21 win over the Academy, which had a coaching staff that included Ken Hatfield, Bill Parcells and current Tech defensive coordinator Al Groh.

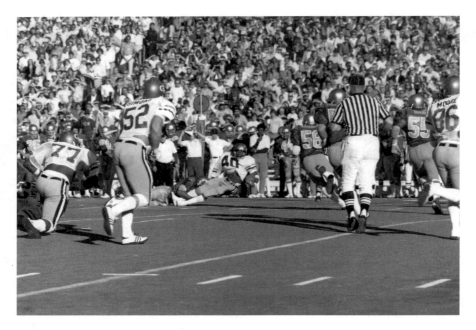

Tech's record setter, Eddie Lee Ivery. *Georgia Tech Athletic Association.*

In below-freezing conditions, and with Ivery throwing up pretty much every time he came off the field, he gave an NCAA record-breaking performance.

Kim King told a story as the team was waiting to leave Colorado Springs in his book *Tales from the Sidelines*:

> *Pepper Rodgers was the Tech coach, and he came up to me and said, "Kim, how much money have you got on you?" Growing up, I never had that much money. One of the things, even to this day, that is consistent with me is that I keep a good bit of money on me. I pulled out my money clip and Pepper grabbed it from me.*
>
> *I said, "What are you doing?" He said, "What am I gonna do with all these kids? I'm gonna find all the beer I can find and we're gonna have a helluva beer party." Pepper found a guy who got us four kegs and set it up in a bar, and we had a beer party.*
>
> *You could never do that now, of course. Nobody got out of hand. Nobody got rowdy. It was just Pepper's way of rewarding the kids while we were waiting to get out of Colorado Springs.*

Ivery finished eighth in the Heisman Trophy voting for the year. But a 4-6-1 season in 1979 meant that Dodd's school had to let his old player go as head coach. Dodd was quoted in the *Sumter (SC) Daily Item* after the firing as thinking that "he [Rodgers] could give us some exposure" since the athletic program felt the Atlanta Braves were hurting the gate. Athletic Director Doug Weaver, and his eventual successor Homer Rice, was moving the school into the Atlantic Coast Conference and needed a fresh face… someone who knew what Tech was all about as the Jackets entered the 1980s.

Erk, GATA and the Junkyard Dawgs

Erskine "Erk" Russell, an Auburn graduate, was an assistant there and at Vanderbilt before heading to Athens to be a part of Vince Dooley's first staff back in 1964—a job that he held for sixteen straight seasons.

Erk was a master motivator who got players to give 100 percent, even if they may not have been the biggest, the best or the most talented or weren't even in the right place on the field. In his seventeen seasons, Russell ran the "Junkyard Dawgs" defense, recording twenty-seven shutouts. One of Russell's most well-known personality traits was head-butting his own players—with their helmets on—to the point that Russell's forehead would open up and bleed during warm-ups.

The acronym GATA can be traced to Russell's coaching tenure. He came up with it one year after playing his hated rivals on North Avenue, seeing their athletic association acronym (GTAA) plastered all over the place. He tweaked the order and came up with "Get After Their Asses." Defenses all over college football use the letters today.

But after the 1974 season, there wasn't a whole lot of GATA. The Bulldogs finished 6-6, with the defense giving up twenty or more points eight times. Russell found motivation in the chorus of the Jim Croce song "Bad, Bad Leroy Brown":

> *And it's bad, bad Leroy Brown*
> *The baddest man in the whole damned town*
> *Badder than old King Kong*
> *And meaner than a junkyard dog*

"I was looking for a name for our defense." Erk Russell said in an interview. "A supporter said, 'Why don't you use Junkyard Dogs?' I didn't think it was original enough, but I couldn't think of anything better, so we went with it." To this day, the Junkyard Dawgs label has been tagged with every Georgia defense.

In Tony Barnhart's book *What It Means to Be a Bulldog*, former Georgia defensive end Dicky Clark said, "Erk was trying to come up with a catchy name to describe what was a pretty scrawny defense. None of us were really big, I think Ronnie Swoopes [at 245 pounds] was the biggest guy we had, and the rest of us barely go to 200 pounds."

The 1975 Junkyard Dawgs appeared in the Cotton Bowl and, in 1976, had a national-best four shutouts and led the SEC in scoring defense by allowing 118 points. The team won the SEC Championship and went to the Sugar Bowl, where it lost to Tony Dorsett and Pitt, 27–3.

The Era of the QB in Athens Begins

Ray Goff led Moultrie High School to an 8-2 record in 1971 and received honorable mention all-state honors. In 1972, Goff quarterbacked the Packers to an undefeated regular season and a 1-AAA Region championship, only the second in school history. Moultrie ended the 1972 regular season number one in the *Atlanta Journal-Constitution* poll but would eventually lose in the state semifinals.

By his sophomore season of 1974 in Athens, Head Coach Vince Dooley had handed the quarterback chores to Goff and Matt Robinson. Goff was the running quarterback and Robinson the passing quarterback, even as both did what the other was assigned to do just as well as their counterpart.

One of the most memorable moments in Goff's Bulldog career occurred at Vanderbilt on October 18, 1975, thanks to some trickery from Head Coach Vince Dooley. While viewing film of the Commodores, UGA offensive line coach Jimmy Vickers noticed that Vanderbilt's defense tended to lose focus in between plays. So, just before the half, down 7–3, the Bulldogs had a second down at the Vanderbilt twenty-six-yard line. Dooley decided to run a "shoestring" play that the Bulldogs had practiced the Thursday before the game. The football was placed on the

Ray Goff in his playing days. *Georgia Athletic Association.*

right hash mark. Goff approached the ball while Vanderbilt was huddled and pretended to tie his shoe. The rest of the Bulldog offense was at the left hash. Goff flipped the football to flanker Gene Washington, who had an easy thirty-six-yard touchdown run.

"The more I thought about it, the less I thought it would work." Goff said.

As a senior, Goff will be remembered for leading Georgia to twenty-seven straight points, leading the Bulldogs to a 41–27 win over Florida. He rushed for 184 yards and three touchdowns and was five for five, passing for two more scores. During his playing career, he was 3-0 against Florida, and that 1976 comeback helped the Bulldogs get the SEC Championship. He would also be named SEC Player of the Year.

After his playing career, he coached at the University of South Carolina, eventually returning to join Vince Dooley's staff and take over for his old coach.

THE 1980S

DOOLEY'S ON A ROLL

Joel Eaves retired as athletic director at the University of Georgia in 1979, and Dooley was appointed his successor. For nine years, Dooley wore both hats, but by 1988 he had moved on to athletic director full time.

After winning Dooley's third SEC Championship in 1976, the Bulldogs dropped to 5-6 in 1977, Dooley's only losing season as head coach. A 9-2-1 rebound in 1978 was followed by a 6-5 campaign in 1979. But the signing of Herschel Walker in 1980 was huge. One of the top tailbacks in the country, Walker was a home-state kid out of Johnson County High School in the town of Wrightsville, where he rushed for more than six thousand yards in his career. The recruiting of Walker was so important that if it meant Vince Dooley was to miss holiday gatherings with his wife, Barbara, and the rest of the clan, so be it. But it wasn't that easy.

Herschel really wanted to be a marine. He had developed from a shy kid who got beaten up and was labeled "special" because of a stutter to someone who had been offered academic scholarships to Harvard and Yale by his senior year—even winning the first-ever Dial Award given to high school scholar-athletes. He did five thousand push-ups and sit-ups each day to stay in shape. But he didn't play football until ninth grade.

Some only need one name to be known: Herschel. *Richard Fowlkes.*

"I knew if I went home after school, I'd have to wash dishes," Herschel told Ron Higgins of the SEC Digital Network. "I hated washing dishes, so I played football."

Herschel's sister was attending the University of Georgia, so a lot of people thought it was a lock that he would follow. He flipped a coin between going to college and the marines—college won. Then he wanted to think of the place Bulldog fans hated most. That would be Clemson.

Herschel would flip a coin to determine Clemson or UGA. Georgia won. He wanted to go "best of five." Georgia won again. Then he flipped between Southern Cal and Georgia. Georgia won again. He then told his mom that he was going to draw out of a hat. Georgia won again—three times.

Herschel's parents called Dooley and told him that their son would sign, but Herschel was joking about it. Dooley showed up, and Walker didn't have the heart to tell him, so he signed. But Dooley didn't think Herschel was ready for the Southeastern Conference.

Walker told Higgins what happened next:

Coach Dooley came up to me and my father and said, "We're happy to have Herschel at the University of Georgia. But we really don't think he can play there. We're happy to have him there, because he's one of the smartest students in the state of Georgia."

All my life, I've heard kids tell me I wasn't good enough. I heard teachers tell me I wasn't good enough. So I began doing more sit-ups, more pushups, ran more. I wanted to be ready to play when I got to Georgia.

The 1980 season is one that Bulldog fans will always remember—from the fourth-teamer from Wrightsville who ran over people in Knoxville to the nail biter over George Rogers and South Carolina to Belue to "Lindsay Scott! Lindsay Scott! Lindsay Scott" to wins over Auburn and Tech to get to the Sugar Bowl. The Bulldogs won them all, won their fourth SEC Championship and beat Notre Dame, 17–10, to claim the undisputed national championship.

After the game, Dooley told *Sports Illustrated* for its January 12, 1981 edition, "I don't know how good we are, but I do know we're 12-0 and nobody else is."

The early 1980s were, record-wise, Dooley's finest moments as head coach. From 1980 to 1983, Georgia was 43-4-1, including three SEC Championships and the national championship. Herschel Walker, the offensive centerpiece, won the Heisman Trophy in 1982 as a junior after finishing second in the voting as a sophomore in 1981 and third as a freshman in 1980.

"I'm going to tell you a secret: the first time I was told that I was up for the Heisman Trophy, I didn't even know what the Heisman Trophy was," Herschel told Higgins with a laugh. "I had to look it up."

Herschel finished his college career after his junior year and headed to the United States Football League, but he would finish his legendary career with twenty-eight 100-yard games during the regular season—twenty-one in his twenty-two games in his final two seasons. He topped 200 yards nine different times in three years. He is still the SEC's all-time rushing leader with 5,259 yards, averaging more than 5 yards per carry along the way. He also averaged more than 159 yards per game and scored forty-nine times.

After that run of runs, Dooley would coach four more years and would decide to step down as head coach following the 1988 season to concentrate on his other duties at the university. But someone wouldn't be around to see it.

Beautiful Eagle Creek

The football program at Georgia Southern College originally existed from 1924 to 1941. B.L. "Crook" Smith coached all but the first five, but the team only had two seasons over .500 after his time up the road at Mercer with the Bears.

Tommy Palmer, then a correspondent for the *Savannah Morning News–Evening Press*, was on the front lines as the school looked into the idea of what it would take and what it would mean to revive the football program. Everything came to a head in January 1981.

The Football Feasibility Committee at Georgia Southern College gave then president Dr. Dale Lick permission to seek $250,000 to get a program started. Lick told Palmer that "the committee was very excited. It's a very simple process—either we get the money to start it or we don't. If the people are willing to put the dollars there, we're going to start it."

The committee was going to try and make sure that the money came from outside sources, not from the school, and Dr. Lick was going to try and make an early Georgia Southern signature: securing the funds from the lower-third of the state.

By April, Lick announced that the funds were there and that the school was going to start play in the fall of 1981. Wins and losses would count the following year. The vote to make it happen was closer than one would think. The Feasibility Committee, with all of its members' different backgrounds, voted yes. The faculty wasn't sold on the idea. But when Dr. Lick reminded them that he had a vote as well, the 2-1 verdict carried the decision.

"We are confident that football can be a self-sustaining program," he admitted to Palmer. "We feel football will not have a negative effect on our other academic or athletic programs at the college." Then athletic director Bucky Wagner didn't have an idea as to who his first head coach would be, but he did admit that he had received one hundred applications for the vacancy.

Three months later, Erk Russell moved from Athens to Statesboro, starting the football program from scratch. In 1981, the Eagles of GSC played a four-game schedule, and Russell's tenacity showed even then.

Nate Hirsch remembered:

> *The first game was against the Florida State JV team. The game was played on a Monday afternoon in Tallahassee. Florida State wound up*

Three seasons at GSC gave Erk a title. *Georgia Southern University Sports Information Department.*

playing a lot of their varsity players who didn't play in their game on Saturday. With all that, the Eagles played a great game, led late in the fourth quarter, before losing. I went down after the game to the locker room to talk with Coach Russell. I told him congrats on a great effort. He replied, "Don't ever congratulate me after a loss. We had them by the gonads and let it get away." Lesson learned. I never tried that again.

Three seasons after Georgia Southern played its first football game, it won its first of three NCAA Division I-AA National Championships in the decade. Erk's motivational ploys in Athens were just as prevalent in the 'Boro—especially when it came to the healing powers of water.

He got his players to believe that the water from a drainage creek near their practice field, what Russell would call "Beautiful Eagle Creek," would help them win. He took the water in a milk jug to all of the Eagles' road playoff games and poured some of the water in an end zone. The Eagles won, and the water from the creek was a liquid of legend.

In 1985, the Eagles won their first but would have to pull off the greatest comeback in Division I-AA (now the Football Championship Series) at the time to do it. Southern was down 22 points in the third quarter to Furman but would come back to win, 44–42. Tracy Ham completed a touchdown pass to Frank Johnson with ten seconds left in the game for the win. Ham finished the game with 419 yards passing and another 90 yards rushing. Johnson caught seven passes for 148 yards, all in the second half. Southern actually scored 38 of its 44 points in the final twenty-two minutes of play.

They went back to back as Ham rushed for 180 yards and three touchdowns and completed twelve of twenty-one passes for 306 yards and another TD to lead the Eagles to a 48–21 win over Arkansas State in Tacoma, Washington. The Indians (now Red Wolves) were the nation's top-ranked defense in Division I-AA, but Georgia Southern gained 603 yards in total offense–almost dead even rushing and passing (297 rushing and 306 passing). Tim Foley also set a championship game record with four field goals.

"I understand this is the first time anybody has won it back to back," Russell admitted after the fact. "When you consider our history, it shouldn't have happened. It was hard to believe last year and it's still hard to believe."

All his teams had done to that point was go 45-15-1 behind Georgia Southern's first first-team all-American in Tracy Ham. The quarterback who ran the "Ham-Bone" to perfection still holds school records in career passing, attempts, completions, yards and touchdowns. He is still first in career total offense yards with 8,969 yards.

After a quarterfinals appearance and a runner-up loss to Furman again in 1988, Raymond Gross was the QB that led the offense to its third title in 1989, going undefeated and beating Stephen F. Austin at Paulson Stadium in Statesboro. Junior Mike Dowis kicked a 20-yard field goal with 1:41 to go for the win. Southern's 15-0 season was the first of its kind in modern-day college football. The Eagles celebrated in front of a record crowd of 25,725 at Paulson. Gross brought the team back from two fourth-quarter deficits and had 216 total yards of offense, while Joe Ross led the rushers with 152 yards on thirty-one carries.

They were just getting started, but Russell retired from the sidelines a champ. Erk Russell passed away in 2006 at the age of eighty. He was memorialized and remembered by the fans and administration of both Georgia and Georgia Southern, along with the Georgia state legislature and football fans around the state. The vision of him perched on the field house patio in the western end zone with a lighted cigar will always be a memory for the Eagles faithful, and he is warmly thought of there and in Athens for his tireless work building first a defense and then an entire program from scratch.

THE HOME OF THE BRAVES

West Georgia had dropped football as a collegiate sport by 1958, but it brought it back to the football-crazy town of Carrollton in 1981. In its second year of existence, it became the second of three schools to be a champ in a different NCAA classification following Georgia and preceding Georgia Southern. It beat Augustana, 14–0, holding its prolific wing-T offense to under one hundred yards on the day. During the year, the team averaged three times that on a weekly basis. Stagg Bowl X is still the lowest-scoring championship game in Division III history. The liberal arts college from Rock Island, Illinois, hadn't lost a regular season game since October 18, 1980, going into that game, and it ran an unbeaten streak of sixty games that started after the loss in Phenix City, Alabama.

West Georgia beat Bishop College, 27–6, in the national semifinals, but *the* game of the 1982 playoffs was the opening rounder with Widener, Pennsylvania.

"They had defeated West Georgia's inaugural team in the '81 playoffs, 10–3; spoiling an undefeated season," recalled West Georgia sports information director Mitch Gray.

The game was played in a quagmire, following heavy rains all week. West Georgia got behind for the first time all season, but rallied to tie the game at the end of regulation, 17–17. Widener scored to begin OT, and then West Georgia answered on a fourth-and-10 pass from David Archer to Rusty Whaley. West Georgia began the second overtime with a fumble, leaving Widener needing but a field goal for the win. Somehow, they missed, forcing a third overtime period. There are still folks in Pennsylvania who think that kick was good, however, the refs didn't agree.

In the third OT, West Georgia scored on the first play on a run by Harold Long and then held Widener on downs to secure the win. Making that game more interesting, at least to me, was the appearance in the press box of Furman Bisher. This game was played the week between the annual Tech-Georgia game, and Bisher wrote his column for Sunday's paper on this game. The one line I remember from that column was him referring to the two grandstands as "jury boxes."

That West Georgia team had four all-Americans on the roster. Archer, who had transferred from Georgia, was a quarterback in Carrollton but

West Georgia gets its title. *University of West Georgia Sports Information Department.*

played safety at the University of Georgia. Archer's claim to fame before the title was when he intercepted the last-second pass against Georgia Tech to win the game for Georgia, 32–31, in 1978. The others were offensive tackle Bruce Pritchett, linebacker Derrick Germaine and defensive end Angelo Snipes, who went from West Georgia to a career in the Canadian Football League and the National Football League that included a season with the Super Bowl champion Washington Redskins.

One interesting aspect of that 1982 season was that Division III games were broadcast nationally as part of the CBS network's contract with the NCAA. With an NFL strike on the horizon and the need for programming, the network sent its main broadcast teams to do four games on one afternoon, broadcast regionally.

"Anybody know what a Millsap is?" CBS analyst Tom Brookshier apparently said in the production meeting. "First they separate me from Pat Summerall, then they give me West Georgia versus Millsaps in Jackson, Mississippi. You think they're trying to tell me something?"

The Southeast would get the West Georgia–Millsaps game, which turned into a showcase for kick returner Lamar West, who scored on runs of ninety-two and ninety-one yards in a 41–6 victory. When *Sports Illustrated*'s William Taaffe asked West about his first TV appearance, he thought about what happened and said, "I don't think they could see me because I'm so small."

Pate, the pride of Fitzgerald, Georgia, was named National Coach of the Year in 1982. He was on the West Georgia sidelines for two more seasons before returning to the school where his coaching career had started twenty-one years before, Hart County High School in the east Georgia town of Hartwell. He made the playoffs six times in his tenure with the Bulldogs, including a semifinals appearance in 1989. Pate retired after an 11-1 season in 1994.

LIFE'S TOUGH ON THE FLATS

Athletic Director Homer Rice's first move was to hire Bill Curry over one of Pepper Rodgers's assistants who also wanted the job—some guy named Spurrier.

But Curry was another player for Bobby Dodd who understood how important successes for student-athletes off the field (and Tech on the field) were for those who followed what went on every day on North Avenue—even if he had no head coaching experience himself. The only bright spot in that first season of 1980 was a 3–3 tie of Notre Dame at Grant Field. Freshman Ken Whisenhunt completed a pass to Jeff Keisler to set up Tech's points and secure the tie against the top-ranked team in the country.

The second year for Curry couldn't have started optimism on campus at any higher a level. The Jackets' Robert Lavette's fourth-quarter touchdown, his second of the day, capped off an eighty-yard drive to upset the Crimson Tide, 24–21. Unfortunately, the team didn't win another game all year—even as it was Georgia Tech's first football win over Alabama since 1962 (and Alabama's first losing season since 1957). The program experienced more ups and downs with years of 6-5 and 3-8, but the "Black Watch" defense, with Ted Roof and Pat Swilling, led to successes in 1984 and 1985. Instead of helmet stickers as a way of rewarding players for good work on the field, defensive coordinator Don Lindsey would put a black stripe down the center of the helmet and convert the "GT" logo from white to black on the sides.

The 6-4-1 1984 team beat Alabama again and Georgia, too, but Curry would have none of the talk that the Jackets had turned a corner with the

Pat Swilling leads the "Black Watch." *Georgia Tech Athletic Association.*

16-6 win over the nineteenth-ranked Tide. "What we don't need right now is for people to start saying that we are a great team because of this game," he told the Associated Press. "It's just a step. It's a small step, no, make that a big step. We hope to have eleven of these steps in our regular season."

The '85 team went all the way to a 9-2-1 record, tying Tennessee in Knoxville, beating Georgia and winning the All-American Bowl in Birmingham, but after a 5-5-1 season, Curry left for Alabama, replacing Ray Perkins, who moved on to the Tampa Bay Buccaneers. Bobby Ross came down to the Flats from Maryland and took the program to a place it hadn't been for almost four decades by the time the 1990s arrived.

DOOLEY RETIRES

Ray Goff's coaching responsibilities included coaching the tight ends and running backs and being recruiting coordinator from 1981 to 1988. Goff was partly responsible for all of the talent that came to Athens for all of its successes in the decade of the 1980s. In 1988, Vince Dooley retired as head coach of the Bulldogs, and the search began for his replacement. Former defensive coordinator Erk Russell was offered the job but turned it down to stay at Georgia Southern. Dick Sheridan, who was the head coach at North Carolina State, was offered the position, and he turned it down.

After Russell and Sheridan turned the job down, the university began looking at the Dooley staff. "They were in a scramble," Goff told Dawgpost. com and Scout.com in 2007. "There were a couple of assistant coaches at Georgia that put in for the job. One was offensive coordinator George Haffner, who was the choice within the coaching staff itself to get the job, but it never happened." That's when Goff went after the vacancy. Much like what happened with Bill Curry down on North Avenue, Goff was offered the head coaching job at Georgia and accepted—with no head coaching experience.

"They've gone out on a limb, there's no doubt about it," Goff told the Associated Press after the announcement. The last guy to be hired as head coach without experience on campus before Dooley? W.S. "Bull" Whitney—just in time for the 1906 season.

Bob Bishop was the head of the search committee. Murray Poole interviewed him to discuss his thirty-year-plus tenure on the board for *Bulldawg Illustrated*, and Bishop admitted that the search was "all messed up":

> *I told him* [Goff] *when we were walking down the hall at 6:30 in the morning, and Chuck Knapp was the president then, "Ray, I hope we're doing you a favor." But we had a bunch of directors on there then and we got along pretty good but the search got entangled a little. When you're searching for a football coach to replace Coach Dooley the world closes in on you, wanting to know what's going on. But I thought Ray was a good football coach then and I still think Ray was a good coach.*

Goff's first Bulldog team in 1989 finished a mediocre 6-6 but, to the satisfaction of the Georgia fans, defeated Florida, 17–10. It would prove to be the only success a Goff-coached Bulldog team would have against the Gators.

THE 1990S

A TITLE ON NORTH AVENUE

The growth of the Yellow Jackets football program under Bobby Ross hit its high point in the 1990 season. Georgia Tech knocked off two ranked opponents in the first half of the year—twenty-fifth-ranked South Carolina and fifteenth-ranked Clemson. A 13–13 tie against North Carolina ended up being the only mark on the right of the win column all season, but the game at Virginia in Charlottesville was the one that everyone circled as then sixteenth-ranked Tech's toughest test to date.

The Cavaliers were coming into the game top-ranked in the first weekend in November and had leads of 10–0 and 28–14 by halftime behind QB Shawn Moore, who set a school record with 344 yards passing on eighteen of twenty-eight completions. Herman Moore caught nine balls for 234 yards and scored off a 63-yard fake reverse to give Virginia a 35–28 lead in the third quarter. But Tech responded with a William Bell run late in the quarter to tie the game again. Tech kicker Scott Sisson and Cavs kicker Jake McInerney swapped kicks to tie the game again at 38 with 2:30 left. But Tech drove 56 yards behind Bell's running (including falling on his own fumble to keep the drive alive) and QB Shawn Jones's completions to Bell and Greg Lester to set up Sisson's game-winning field goal with seven seconds left for a 41–38 win at Scott Stadium. The game is regarded as one of the best in the history of the ACC and catapulted Tech to seventh in the country.

"We felt like we could score on their defense," Bell admitted after the game. "And that's what we came out and did." Shawn Jones told then WAGA-TV sports director Jeff Hullinger in a postgame interview that he didn't know what to say, initially, "but I can say this: we're bringing a championship back to Atlanta."

The 13-point underdogs then knocked off Virginia Tech, Wake Forest and Georgia to set up a New Year's Day matchup in the Citrus Bowl with nineteenth-ranked Nebraska. Tech had taken leads of 21–0 and 24–14 by the half. After blocking a field goal in the third quarter, Tech took a 31–14 lead before the Huskers scored again to make it 31–21, but the Jackets scored twice for the 45–21 win. The victory gave Tech an 11-0-1 record, and when the Coaches Poll (UPI) was released the following day, the Jackets were on top of half of the college football world.

The 10–9 Colorado win over Notre Dame in the Orange Bowl split the national title with the Buffaloes and caused some consternation among those who wanted to remind everyone that it took a fifth-down conversion for Colorado to beat Missouri and that Bill McCartney's team tied Tennessee and lost at Illinois. A late Rocket Ismail touchdown was even called back in the Orange Bowl due to a clipping call to help preserve the win.

Bobby Ross restored Georgia Tech to Bobby Dodd success levels for the school's second national title. He was never able to follow that level of work, but the next year resulted in an eight-win season and Ross moved on to the San Diego Chargers. The rest of the decade, however, was marked with inconsistency at the beginning and a Heisman hopeful by the end.

Bill Lewis was hired away from East Carolina, but he was nowhere close to Ross's successes in his first two years—winning five games each year. For 1994, George O'Leary was brought back as defensive coordinator. But injuries to both quarterbacks, Donnie Davis and Tom Luginbill, sent the team to a 1-7 start, and Lewis was fired midseason. O'Leary took over for the balance of that year and was named head coach for 1995. As O'Leary tried to have his team recover from Lewis's failed ideas, he found a young quarterback who got the program national attention over the last three years of the decade: Joe Hamilton.

South Carolina's high school Player of the Year in some circles, the graduate of Macedonia High School brought a dual threat to Ralph Friedgen's offense. Hamilton started in 1997 and led Tech to its first bowl in six years: the 1997 Carquest Bowl. In 1998, Tech won ten games and beat

Notre Dame in the Gator Bowl. Hamilton was a leading candidate for the Heisman Trophy his senior year, up against Wisconsin's Ron Dayne. His 3,700-plus yards of total offense led to him being runner-up in the voting.

Hamilton ended up alternating among limited duty in the NFL, NFL Europe and Arena Football before leaving the playing field, taking a position with the fledgling Georgia State football program under Bill Curry. But Hamilton's place in Tech lore is locked in place. And, if you look hard enough, you may find one of those mouse pads the school released to promote his Heisman Trophy senior season.

WHILE HAMILTON WAS CLOSE

A school in South Georgia was racking up the hardware in Division II. Valdosta State's Blazers had a high-powered offense under Hal Mumme, who took over for Mike Cavan. Mumme had picked up district Coach of the Year honors in two of his three seasons at Iowa Wesleyan College and had taken the team to its first-ever playoff berths while leading the NAIA in passing offense. The offense translated to Valdosta with a quarterback, Chris Hatcher, out of the Mount de Sales school in Macon by 1994. In that year, "Hatch" helped lead his team to its first-ever playoff berth as well and win the Harlon Hill Trophy (the Division II version of the Heisman) by the second-largest vote margin in the history of the award. Hatcher won the award after throwing for 4,076 yards, fifty-five touchdowns and only ten interceptions. Hatcher led the country in passing efficiency during the regular season as the Blazers made the quarterfinals.

After dropping to a 6-5 record as the team transitioned out of the Chris Hatcher era, Lance Funderburke, Hatcher's successor, took the team to the second round of the postseason again and garnered runner-up honors for the Harlon Hill. He completed more than 64 percent of his passes for thirty-eight touchdowns, with only fourteen interceptions. His 4,226 yards passing on the year were both Valdosta State and Gulf South Conference records.

Mumme left after the 1996 season to take over at Kentucky. Mike Kelly succeeded him, but it took Hatch to return out of uniform and work on the sidelines for the Blazers to take the next step on their championship quests in Division II.

Georgia's Long Decade

It could actually be attributed to the only time in modern history that neither the chain link fencing nor the hedges could keep fans off the field at Sanford Stadium. The October 7, 2000 win over Tennessee was a celebration that turned out to be one that was few and far between during the 1990s. Ray Goff's ten wins in his first two seasons, combined with the 1990 national championship at Georgia Tech, didn't make the Bulldog faithful feel any better about themselves.

The emergence of Marietta High grad Eric Zeier helped out early on. Zeier took over as quarterback midway through the 1991 season, and the Bulldogs finished 9-3, defeating Arkansas, 24–15, at the Independence Bowl. They started the 1992 season at 7-1 before losing to Florida in Jacksonville. The Bulldogs did defeat Auburn (when the defense "saved our what-cha-ma-call-its" according to the legendary voice of the Bulldogs, Larry Munson), Georgia Tech and Ohio State in the Citrus Bowl to create some off-season optimism for 1993. That's all it turned out to be.

The Bulldogs got off to a 4-4 start heading into the Florida game. It looked like Georgia would tie the game when Eric Zeier hit Jerry Jerman on a twelve-yard touchdown pass, but Anthone Lott had called time out and the touchdown was wiped off the board. Georgia eventually lost to Florida, Auburn and Georgia Tech to finish the year 5-6. Goff was on thin ice.

In 1994, it got worse after a 6-4-1 year with losses to Vandy in Athens, a blow-out loss to Florida (52–14) and an equally bad loss to Tech (48–10 in Athens). Zeier was one of the few bright spots during those years, and by the time he graduated, he had his name attached to sixty-seven Georgia passing records and eighteen SEC records. By 1995, however, after losing to Alabama, Florida putting up fifty-two in Athens and Auburn winning at Sanford Stadium did him in. Public Enemy No. 1 for UGA fans, Steve Spurrier, told the assembled media after the game, "I heard no one ever hung half a hundred on Georgia"...so he did.

After the Auburn loss, Athletic Director Vince Dooley fired his former quarterback and present coach. When asked about his tenure as a coach, Goff was happy about his work on the sidelines. "I am proud of what we accomplished at Georgia," Goff told DawgPost.com and Scout.com in 1997. "We didn't win every game, but we had good kids."

For Georgia fans, the news got worse, even if it was symbolic in nature. The treasured hedges would have to be removed for the 1996

Olympics. Dimensions for the soccer competition were wider than the American football field that had been there for seventy years, so they had to go—even if it was divulged later that they had to be treated for disease. And they would have a new coach to finish the decade, or at least they thought they would.

Vince Dooley contacted Glen Mason at Kansas, and following the Aloha Bowl, the Jayhawks' head coach announced that he was leaving to be the new head coach at Georgia. By his own admission, though, something was bugging him about his decision. His head was telling him one thing, and his gut was telling him something else. Mason ended up listening to his gut. A week after announcing that he was leaving, he changed his mind and decided to stay in Lawrence.

"I made this decision last night before I went to bed, and I slept great [Sunday] night," Mason said after the bowl. "I woke up rather early and had the same thing in my mind that I did last night and said, 'I'm going to do it.' Then I looked myself in the mirror and I could tell you, I don't know when I felt as good as I felt [yesterday]." His Jayhawks beat UCLA after hearing the news.

"First of all, I want to apologize to the University of Georgia," he continued, "especially to Coach Dooley. I think I probably put them in an embarrassing situation. I don't like to put anyone in an embarrassing position and I'm not normally a guy who waffles on a decision. But in the week that I took the [Georgia] job, I thought it over—what was in the best interest of my family and me personally. I didn't think I'd feel as bad as I do. But life goes on and I'm going to go on and take it from here."

Dooley, in turn, released a statement: "I was very disappointed and asked him to reconsider; however, he was determined to stay at Kansas." Dooley acted swiftly and brought in Jim Donnan, the head coach of Division I-AA powerhouse Marshall, to replace Mason, who was supposed to replace Goff.

"I can't say how excited I am about what I consider the opportunity of a lifetime," Donnan said in a statement after he was hired. "Georgia has one of the richest football traditions in the country and it also gives me the chance to return to my roots in the South."

While there were individuals who made their names in Bulldog lore like Hines Ward, Robert Edwards, Kirby Smart, "Champ" Bailey, Matt Stinchcomb, Quincy Carter and Richard Seymour, the numbers in Donnan's columns can be looked at two ways. He improved Goff's teams to finish the decade 10-2, 9-3 and 8-4 after a 5-6 in year one.

Donnan's teams only went 2-2 against Auburn. He won one of the most exciting games in the history of the Auburn rivalry in 1996. The "Miracle on the Plains" was the first game in the history of the SEC to go to overtime. Mike Bobo completed a touchdown pass to Cory Allen as UGA won 56–49 in four overtimes. It was also the game during which the UGA V tried to get a piece of Auburn wide receiver Robert Baker on the sidelines. But Tommy Tuberville got his first big win in 1999 as an underdog.

Donnan would be remembered for skipping across the field at Jacksonville Municipal Stadium when Georgia won only one of four times in the rivalry since 1990 behind the running of Robert Edwards. But his teams only won that game in the decade against the Gators. He did not beat Tennessee in the 1990s and only went 2-2 against Georgia Tech, and Donnan's teams never won the SEC title. The Bulldogs even lost to all four of these rivals in 1999.

Hines Ward's numbers (149 catches and 1,965 yards) put him second in team history at the time, and his 3,870 all-purpose yards is still second to Herschel Walker. In 1997, Hines was named an all-SEC performer as a precursor to his successes in the National Football League.

But for Donnan and the Dogs, wins were one thing, and big wins were an entirely different thing altogether. And they weren't happening at a pace fans desired.

STATESBORO KEEPS ROLLING

When Erk Russell was hired to start the Georgia Southern football program, the school actually had to buy a football for placement at the first news conference. Tim Stowers didn't have to worry about that. After the 1989 championship, Russell retired from the sidelines, and the thirty-two-year-old, six-year assistant got to live out his dream and dream job replacing a man he called the "greatest football coach ever." The biggest change for the new head coach was that, other than having to do the administrative work he didn't do as an assistant, his wife didn't have to work anymore—a fact not lost on the soon-to-be father of two.

He kept the same open-door policy as his predecessor, and the senior leaders on the Eagles squad knew what was happening in Statesboro. "Coach Russell and Coach Stowers are two of the last of the old-time coaches," defensive end Giff Smith told Anthony Stasny of the *Savannah News-Press* before the 1990 season. "He has that gruff voice and that swagger. They concentrate more on motivating people than on strategy, not that they don't know their Xs and Os. But they are the kind of guys who can take two average players and put them together and come up with something way above average."

The 1990 season started with a lot of uncharacteristic adjustment for the preseason number one team in the country. The Eagles beat Valdosta State but lost to Middle Tennessee, Florida State and Eastern Kentucky to go 1-3. That would be the end of the losing.

The team, led by QB Raymond Gross and running back Joe Ross, ended up with the school's fourth title in the past six seasons with a 36–13 performance over Nevada. Gross ran for 145 yards on the day, and Ross finished the year with more than 1,100 yards rushing on the season for the team that wrapped the year 13-2. Rebuilding followed with two 7-4 seasons after the fourth title, but the Eagles made their way back to the quarterfinals with a 10-3 mark in 1993. Stowers only coached for two more seasons in Statesboro, wrapping with another 9-4 mark in 1995.

Athletic Director Sam Baker fired Stowers after the 1995 season without seeing him coach a game on the sidelines and brought in Senior Associate Athletic Director Frank Ellwood as an interim coach for 1996. Ellwood lasted just the one season, the first losing season in Georgia Southern's modern history, at 4-7.

PAUL JOHNSON RETURNS

Paul Johnson never played college football. He had gone from a high school coach to a head coach at Lees-McRae Junior College in Banner Elk, North Carolina. From Lees-McRae, Johnson made his first tour at Georgia Southern as a line coach and then as offensive coordinator. In 1985, he was the one who convinced Erk Russell to run the flexbone offense.

"We were run-and-shoot, and he wanted to move to an I formation," Johnson told *Sports Illustrated*'s Albert Chen in 2009. "I told him [Russell], 'We don't have a tight end, we don't have a fullback. Let's try this.' Fifteen minutes later he came back to me and said, 'Do what you have to do.'"

After all the record numbers the school put on the score sheets, Johnson traveled all the way to Hawaii to be the Warriors' offensive coordinator and

Paul Johnson continues Southern's success. *Georgia Southern University Sports Information Department.*

AP came close versus UMass. *Georgia Southern University Sports Information Department.*

then to the Naval Academy for two years at the same position. In 1997, he returned to Statesboro to start another Eagles run to the top of Division I-AA. In Johnson's first year, the Eagles returned to the playoffs, losing in the quarterfinals. But in 1998, behind the running of Adrian Peterson, the team made it all the way back to the national title game, losing to UMass. In 1999, the 'Boro had another title trophy on campus. The 13-2 team only lost in a 48–41 shootout in Corvallis, Oregon, to Oregon State and 17–16 to Appalachian State in Boone, North Carolina.

Adrian Peterson finished the season with 2,704 yards rushing—247 of them would come against Youngstown State in the finale against a Penguins team that only gave up an average of 166 yards per game. His twenty-five-carry performance would go down in the NCAA record books (as well as the 638-yard team rushing performance). The Eagles' 59–24 win gave the team its fifth title, the most in Division I-AA history. Quarterback Greg Hill ran for 1,529 yards himself and added 1,461 through the air on the year, and Peterson received the Walter Payton Award for his efforts as the Most Outstanding Player in I-AA.

Johnson and the Eagles weren't done.

THE TWENTY-FIRST CENTURY

THE EAGLES CONTINUE THEIR DOMINANCE

Top-ranked for seven weeks of the regular season as defending champs, Johnson and his three-headed monster of Peterson (2,056 yards and nineteen touchdowns), quarterback J.R. Revere (sixteen touchdowns) and running back Mark Myers rushed for more than 3,600 yards, while Revere found wide receiver Chris Johnson for almost 1,000 yards receiving and ten of Revere's thirteen passing scores. A Southern Conference loss to Elon would knock Georgia Southern to number six in the country leading into the playoffs, but wins over McNeese, Hofstra and Delaware would set up a title game with Montana in Chattanooga, Tennessee, where the Eagles would battle the Griz for the full sixty minutes.

"A.P." WOULD NOT DISAPPOINT

Southern led 20–3 in the third quarter, but the Grizzlies mounted a furious comeback to lead 23–20. Peterson scored from 57 yards out to regain the lead and finished the day with 148 yards on the ground as Johnson put the sixth title on the Statesboro mantle. The 2001 season was his last as head coach. After a semifinals appearance and eight more weeks ranked number one in the country, the Eagles fell short of another championship with a loss to conference rival Furman.

Johnson's high-powered offense traveled to Navy and turned around the Middies, and it could be argued that his years rank only second to those of Erk Russell when it comes to the program's evolution and overall success.

Offensive coordinator Mike Sewak succeeded Johnson with a semifinals run of his own in 2002, but he only took the team to the first round of the playoffs in two other postseason turns. He was dismissed three days after the team blew a 19-point lead in a 50–35 first-round Division I-AA playoff loss to Texas State in 2005. But the acrimony with Sewak dated back to the 2003 season when the Eagles failed to make the playoffs altogether. Sewak fired defensive coordinator Rusty Russell, son of former Georgia Southern coach Erk Russell. From that moment, Erk Russell cut all ties to the program.

"When we hired Paul Johnson, I remember him saying there was a time when Georgia Southern was feared," GSU athletic director Sam Baker said at the press conference announcing the dismissal. "When Paul was hired, we weren't. When he left, we were feared again. I'm not so sure we're not back to being not feared."

A search was held to bring in a successor to make the Eagles feared, and the new coach didn't necessarily need to run the triple-option. Brian VanGorder didn't, but the program was rocked by the death of Erk Russell the day before the 2006 season opener against Central Connecticut.

Russell had only spoken to the team the day before for a pep talk, and according to officials in Statesboro, he apparently had a stroke while behind the wheel of his car. VanGorder wanted to bring Erk back into the fold, and the idea of the talk struck the right notes. Donald Heath of the *Savannah Morning News* tracked down former Eagles to ask about what Heath described as Russell having "it."

"He taught the game of football, but it wasn't until later in life that you realized he was teaching you something that could be applied in everyday life," said Eagles former kicker Terry Harvin. "His favorite saying was, 'Just One More Time.' That's what you think every day you wake up."

"I think everyone is going to miss him," said Navy coach Paul Johnson. "I don't know anyone who didn't like him. He gave me a chance to get started. I probably owe almost everything to him. Not many people could have done what he did at Georgia Southern."

The Eagles got their title in 2001. *Georgia Southern University Sports Information Department.*

Regrettably, the VanGorder season turned out to be a disaster at 3-8, including losing the last five in a row, and he left in favor of Chris Hatcher, who had turned his alma mater into a force in Division II. But Hatcher couldn't seem to get his high-powered, pass-happy offense to stick, and he gave way to Jeff Monken for the 2010 season. Monken was Paul Johnson's special teams coordinator on the Flats and was asked by Athletic Director Sam Baker to take his first head coaching opportunity in Statesboro.

Monken had always wanted to be a head coach, and the chance was too good to pass up. "Anybody that coaches there realizes that…Ga. Southern is a school that people hold in high regard among FCS schools," he told the *Atlanta Journal-Constitution*'s Doug Roberson. "The last couple of decades, it's one of the most successful programs in the country. Tremendous to be considered and grateful for the opportunity."

His first years in the 'Boro have given fans and alums alike reasons for optimism. Two semifinals appearances will do that for a program that looks to return to being feared. But from the plain-looking, blue-and-white uniforms that started out as a financial necessity to traveling to games in yellow school buses to Freedom flights, singing the "Valley Song" and "Hugo Bowl," the bald-headed coach who wanted a challenge left an indelible mark on a program that he still watches over today. It's just in the form of a bronze bust in the western end zone now.

NEXT STOP: VALDOSTA

Chris Hatcher took over the program as head coach and made sure that his offense would garner national attention. In the first year, every win by the Blazers lighted up the scoreboard. The team scored less than forty-two only once. Five wins were in the forties, and four wins were in the fifties. Junior quarterback Dusty Bonner won the Harlon Hill Trophy for the 10-2 team. He tied Hatcher's Blazer and Gulf South Conference mark of fifty-five touchdown passes and threw for more than 4,100 yards.

The next year, Bonner became the second player in Division II to win the Hill back to back, throwing for a little over four thousand yards while completing more than 70 percent of his passes and fifty-two touchdowns. The playoffs would become commonplace for VSU, with a first-round run followed by a national runner-up finish in 2002. Grand Valley State scored with a little over a minute to play for the win as the Blazers finished 14–1.

Another 10-2 year in 2003 was the setup for the school's first title in 2004, a 36–31 win over Pittsburg State. Quarterback Fabian Walker transferred from Florida State, ending up not far from his childhood home in Americus, to guide the team to the win in Florence, Alabama. The "Black Swarm" defense kept the Gorillas in check. The Blazers actually lost their season-opening game against Albany State and proceeded to run the table.

After 9-3 and 8-2 seasons, Hatcher took the opening in Statesboro and gave way to longtime offensive coordinator David Dean. Dean's team made an instant impression with a title in 2007—a 25–20 win over Northwest Missouri State. The so-called Cardiac Kids pulled off their fourth straight second-half come-from-behind victory as Valdosta State defeated Northwest Missouri State, 25–20, and as Michael Terry scored with twenty-two seconds left in regulation.

Since the second title in school history, the competitiveness of the Gulf South Conference has shown its Division II supremacy as the Blazers have gone 9-3, 6-4, 8-3 and 6-4, even with the separation of the Arkansas, Texas and Oklahoma schools. Meanwhile, Delta State and North Alabama have ascended to the national title game appearances.

GEORGIA MILITARY COLLEGE

Former head coach Lew Cordell died in 2002, but he honored GMC with an estate gift of more than $700,000 to the GMC Foundation "for the support and enhancement of the Georgia Military College athletic program."

Georgia Military College had gone without football for more than twenty years when the decision was made to return the sport to the Milledgeville campus for the 1991 season. Glenn Wolfe was selected as head coach to revive the storied football program, though he retired from coaching after his first year at GMC. Robert Nunn, Oklahoma State standout and defensive coordinator for Coach Wolfe, was selected to lead the program, which he did with great success for eight years, going through the 1999 season and earning five bowl berths over his eight years. Coach Nunn left GMC for the NFL, where he has worked for Miami, Washington, Green Bay and Tampa Bay and currently is a Super Bowl champion with the New York Giants.

Since the program was reinstated in 1991, the school has sent 274 athletes to Division I schools and another 137 to Division II schools (the most of any school), and 2 (Odell Thurman and Derrick Wimbush) were named to the 2005 NFL All-Rookie Team; 19 more eventually made their way to the NFL with Williams as their head coach. But the program has been one of the premier programs in all of the junior college ranks, winning the NJCAA National Championship in 2001 over Butler (Kansas) and being runner-up in 2002 (against Joliet Junior College) and again in 2005. Since 1994, the Bulldogs have finished their season ranked thirteen times, appearing in twelve postseason bowl games, producing fifty-nine all-Americans and a Hall of Fame head coach in Bert Williams—head coach since 2000 and offensive coordinator for Nunn from 1997 to 1999.

Commented GMC Head Coach Bert Williams:

> *GMC has a long, long history with football in the state of Georgia. Well known greats like Wally Butts, Bill Hartman and Georgia Sports Hall of Fame inductee Lew Cordell got their starts here in the glory days, and countless young men have gotten their second chances in life here since the resumption of football in 1991. We have had some football greats as well—we had both a player and coach earn Super Bowl Rings the last two years for example—but our proudest achievement has been sending 25–30 young men into four-year colleges and universities each year and helping them move forward in life.*

Williams and his staff are more than proud of all the accomplishments in the last dozen years or so, making sure that the experience is about the student-athlete being well rounded.

THE RICHT ERA BEGINS

Quincy Carter was Jim Donnan's quarterback for the 2000 season, but the head coach went after a kid from South Gwinnett High School to be his next signal-caller.

In Tony Barnhart's book *What It Means to Be a Bulldog*, Greene shared that he wasn't all that highly recruited, "but coach Donnan seemed to see something in me that I really didn't see in myself. In my dealings with him, he gave me the confidence that I could be a good player if I worked at it."

Donnan wouldn't be around to see it. Mark Richt took over as head coach in 2001 and, before the season began, named red-shirt freshman David Greene as the starting quarterback before the season-opener with Arkansas State over Cory Phillips. Greene led the Bulldogs to an 8-4 record and a Music City Bowl bid and was named the Southeastern Conference's Offensive Freshman of the Year.

In 2002, Greene led Georgia to the SEC Championship game against Arkansas. Greene threw for 237 yards and was named the game's Most Valuable Player as Georgia routed Arkansas, 30–3. It was the Bulldogs' first SEC Championship since 1982. In 2003, Georgia wrapped up a 10-2 season with an SEC Eastern Division Championship. Greene threw a career-high 3,307 yards, leading the Bulldogs back to Atlanta for the SEC Championship game. But an LSU team headed for a national championship beat UGA, 34–13. Greene ended up as MVP in the Capital One Bowl, throwing for 327 yards against Purdue as the Bulldogs defeated the Boilermakers, 34–27.

Though the 2004 season ended without an SEC Championship, Greene ended his Georgia career leading the Bulldogs to a 24–21 Outback Bowl win over Wisconsin, and his name ended up all over the Bulldogs' record books. He became only the second quarterback in Georgia history to start all four years (John Rauch was Georgia's starting quarterback from 1944 to 1948). His forty-two wins as Georgia's starting quarterback was an NCAA record (broken by Texas's Colt McCoy in 2009). His 214 consecutive pass completions in 2004 is an SEC record, and David Greene ended his college career as the SEC's all-time career leader in yards gained with 11,270. His childhood friend, David Pollack, patrolled the defense during those years.

By the time the Shiloh High School student was done, Pollack would be voted one of the College Football Players of the Decade by *Sports*

Illustrated. He was a three-time all-American. The only other Bulldog to do that is Herschel Walker. He won the Ted Hendricks Award for the best Collegiate Defensive End twice. He was the 2002 SEC Player of the Year during a year when the Bulldogs won the SEC title and beat Florida State in the Sugar Bowl, and he was named 2004 SEC Defensive Player of the Year.

But the single play that people associate with Pollack is his theft of a Corey Jenkins pass attempt during the South Carolina game in 2002. Jenkins was in his follow through, and Pollack reached around, grabbed the ball and ended up with a touchdown against South Carolina. Pollack finished up his career with a school-record thirty-six sacks before pursuing a career in the NFL and, now, television.

DAMON EVANS TAKES OVER

By the age of thirty-four, the Gainesville High School grad had taken over as athletic director at the University of Georgia. University president Michael Adams decided to remove Vince Dooley as athletic director, much to the dismay of many alums and fans in 2004, in a move portrayed as putting a legend out to pasture in a legendary power struggle since Dooley's contract wouldn't be renewed. Dooley, in turn, handpicked Evans as his successor.

Dooley said at the time, "I said often that it seemed just a short time ago that I was in his living room talking to his mother, father and Damon about the great opportunities that he would have here at Georgia if he came. Little did I know at the time that the opportunities would include one day succeeding me as athletic director. He has done a splendid job of building on the program that he inherited."

Evans was a four-year starting wide receiver in Athens graduating in 1992 and got his master's degree from UGA. He worked his way up from a position at SEC Headquarters to, eventually, making his way back to Georgia. Evans was up front in the efforts for the new Stegeman Coliseum practice facility and the expansion of the Butts-Mehre Athletic Buildings. But his downfall was just as quick as his ascent.

Evans stepped down in July 2010 after being charged with DUI in Atlanta. A twenty-eight-year-old female passenger in Evans's car was arrested for disorderly conduct. The married father of two told the arresting officer he was Georgia's athletic director, trying to get him to acquiesce in some manner, according to the arrest report from the Georgia State Patrol.

"I let this university down. I let my family down. I let those in the Bulldog Nation down. I let so many people down that have supported me and believed in me along the way," Evans said at the press conference the day after his arrest. "I sincerely apologize for my actions. I hope you find it in your hearts to forgive me. I'm an individual who made a grave, grave mistake that will be with me for the rest of my life."

President Adams brought in Greg McGarity from the University of Florida after a detailed search to take over the athletic director position to oversee the continued revenue successes of a top-ten overall program.

DAVID YIELDS TO D.J.

D.J. Shockley was heavily recruited out of North Clayton High School, where he played for his father. Mark Richt kept the Georgia star as one of his first recruits, but he bided his time behind David Greene. He was thought of so highly that even as he got some reps in games, he might have done better to transfer if he had wanted to get a starting job. D.J. never left.

In 2005, the Bulldogs had to figure out how to replace David Pollack on defense and David Greene on offense. Shockley came out in his first game and threw for five touchdowns against Boise State. The Dogs started the season 7-0 and were ranked fourth in the country. However, in that seventh win against Arkansas, Shockley left with a sprained knee and couldn't play in the loss to Florida. He returned for the Auburn loss, but they clinched the SEC East title with a 45–13 win over Kentucky and blew out LSU in the SEC Championship game for a Sugar Bowl berth.

The Bulldogs secured their third Eastern Division title in four years, but this Sugar Bowl was special for a different reason. Hurricane Katrina had devastated the city of New Orleans, and the Sugar Bowl Committee was looking for another location for the game with West Virginia. Atlanta and the Georgia Dome filled in.

Shockley threw three more touchdowns in the Sugar Bowl, tying Eric Zeier's record of twenty-four touchdown passes in a season in a year when the Bulldogs surprised everyone with their on-field performance. West Virginia went out to a 28–0 lead early in the game, but Shockley led a furious comeback only to lose, 38–35, behind Steve Slaton's 204 yards rushing.

But D.J. Shockley's place was solidified as someone who stayed home and stayed a Bulldog—counting their win over Virginia Tech in the Chick-fil-A Bowl, the Dogs finished 9-4 in 2006. Joe Tereshinski III was supposed to be the quarterback, but Matt Stafford had taken over by week two after an injury to JT3. Stafford came from Dallas, Texas, and Highland Park High School. But the season was also responsible for one of Larry Munson's last, signature calls when Georgia upset sixteenth-ranked Georgia Tech.

When Stafford hit Mohamed Massaquoi for the game-winning score, Munson screamed, "My God! Massaquoi!" and the Bulldogs knocked off the Jackets for their second upset in a row, having beaten fifth-ranked Auburn two weeks before. And that set the Bulldogs up for 2007.

THE KID FROM NEW JERSEY

Knowshon Moreno's SAT prep tutor just had a daughter graduate from the University of Georgia. She knew that two of her students, Moreno and lineman Kade Weston, wanted to play football in warmer places and recommended the school. But when it came to attending a camp at UGA between his junior and senior years, Moreno had to take a train since he was too young to fly by himself—sixteen hours' worth of travel.

His Middletown South high school team won its third straight state title his senior year, and he finished with the second-most rushing yards in New Jersey state high school history. The decision came down to Georgia, Virginia Tech and Florida.

After red-shirting his freshman year in 2006, he was sprung onto the SEC halfway through the 2007 season in the game against Vanderbilt. Five straight 100-yard-plus rushing performances later, his 1,334 yards were good enough for second all-time in UGA history for yards gained by a freshman—second to someone named Herschel.

Moreno picked up all-SEC freshman team honors in three separate polls, and he was even named Freshman Offensive Player of the Year by the *Sporting News*. He was also the first freshman since Herschel Walker to gain one hundred yards or more in five straight games.

Georgia returned to a postseason game at the Georgia Dome facing Virginia Tech in the Chick-fil-A Bowl. The Bulldogs won that one, 31–24, over the Hokies. Moreno's sophomore year was more of the same. He was named to seven preseason all-American teams and preseason all-SEC by seven more voting groups. But the signature move that every Bulldog fan associates with Moreno came in week two against Central Michigan when Moreno hurdled Chippewa defensive back Vince Agnew.

The play call, by FoxSportsNet's Bob Rathbun, was a simple, "Look at him jump the defender!" followed by twelve seconds of laughter. The video is a YouTube favorite for Bulldogs fans, having been seen over 230,000 times. He wrapped up the year with an even 1,400 yards and sixteen rushing touchdowns. He became the second Bulldog rusher to go over 1,000 yards in back-to-back seasons (second to Herschel Walker). The 1,400 yards were good enough for a top five in the Georgia record book as well.

Moreno was named a semifinalist for the Maxwell Award and a finalist for the Doak Walker Award and got his name attached to either first- or second-team all-American lists. He declared early for the NFL draft after that season and was drafted by the Denver Broncos, but he will always be on the "best of" list when it comes to tailbacks.

The Bulldogs team of 2007 kind of snuck up on people and just kept winning early, starting out 4-1. But after a loss to Tennessee, the team already had two losses in the SEC East and looked to be out of contention for any major bowl game. But after a last-second win over Vanderbilt and the entire team celebrating on the field against Florida in Jacksonville for only the second time in a decade, next up was Auburn in Athens. Word was that the team was going to dress out in black uniforms. For the CBS broadcast, the entire fan base dressed out (or painted themselves) in the same color and went berserk when the team came out in the new colors after pregame warm-ups.

The game wasn't even close, 45–20 Georgia. And in the week of AC/DC's "Back in Black" during introductions and Soulja Boy blaring out over the public address between the third and fourth quarters, the Bulldogs kept rolling. Finishing the season with wins over Kentucky and Georgia Tech put them at 10-2 and ranked number six.

Tennessee was going to play in the Florida Citrus Bowl as the loser in the SEC Championship game. LSU was going to the BCS title game, and that left the Sugar Bowl to take an SEC team with an at-large bid. They picked Georgia to play Hawaii, another at-large competitor. The Bulldogs plowed the Warriors, 41–10, to finish the season with their seventh straight win, an 11-2 record and a final ranking of second in the AP Poll and third in the Coaches Poll.

Marcus Howard was voted game MVP with three quarterback sacks and two fumbles caused, one of which he recovered for a touchdown. After the game, Warriors quarterback Colt Brennan was heard asking, "Who was that guy?" If only he knew ahead of time.

Summerville High (South Carolina) wide receiver AJ Green always wanted to be a Georgia Bulldog. He committed to the school early on in his high school career and followed through on it. Green teamed with Mohamed Massaquoi to give UGA two deep threats.

Four games into his freshman season, Green, in front of a national television audience, had eight catches for 159 yards and a touchdown versus Arizona State. He led the entire SEC in receiving yards and was the SEC Freshman of the Year in 2008. He set a freshman record at Georgia with fifty-six catches, 963 yards and eight touchdowns. Green was a national semifinalist for the Biletnikoff Award as the nation's best wide receiver as a sophomore and even blocked a game-winning field goal attempt in the Arizona State game that the Bulldogs eventually won, 20–17. The year 2009 was a tough one for both the Bulldogs and for Green. Injured most of the season, AJ still made fifty-three catches for 808 yards and six touchdowns. But after three years, it was time for the Summerville native to leave. He was drafted by the Cincinnati Bengals and is making his mark in the pros.

MATT STAFFORD

The constant in all of the offense outbursts in the late 2000s was this Texas-born quarterback. As a high school senior, Matt Stafford led his team to the Texas Class AAAA state championship—the school's first state title since

1957. He earned EA Sports National High School Player and Texas Player of the Year honors and was nominated the nation's number one quarterback by Rivals.com.

Stafford battled with Joe Cox for the starting role in his freshman year of 2006 but won the Chick-fil-A Bowl's Offensive Most Valuable Player honor by the time he was through. In 2007, Stafford had five games in which he threw for more than 200 yards, but his best year was 2008. Stafford threw for more than 200 yards seven times, but his best performance as a Bulldog came in his final regular season game against archrival Georgia Tech—407 yards and five touchdowns in the 45–42 loss. Stafford ended 2008 with a Capital Bowl MVP performance in the Bulldogs' 24–12 win over Michigan State.

Stafford's 7,731 career passing yards are third all-time at UGA, and the twenty-five touchdowns from his junior season are still a school record. He entered the NFL draft after that performance and became the top pick overall for the Detroit Lions, following in the footsteps of another Highland Park high school grad, Bobby Layne.

The 2010 and 2011 seasons brought a lot more attention to Coach Mark Richt as the fan base wonders, on some level, if there need to be changes at the top. Early losses in the seasons seemed to be tempered by performances as the seasons went along, and when the "Dream Team" was recruited on National Signing Day, optimism was renewed all over again.

Case in point is the 2011 year, when some wanted Richt fired after losses to Boise State and South Carolina. The Bulldogs went on a tear, winning ten before losing to LSU in the SEC title game and an overtime loss to Michigan State in the Outback Bowl.

The year 2012 and beyond will be interesting, to say the least.

FOR GEORGIA TECH, IT WOULD TAKE A WHILE

In 2000, with George O'Leary as head coach, the decade seemed to get off to an odd start when the season opener was suspended from lightning strikes and torrential rains in Blacksburg, Virginia, shown nationally on ESPN, with one strike even hitting Lee Corso's rental car in the parking lot. The Yellow Jackets, after starting 2-2, won seven in a row, including the annual Georgia game, but lost their bowl game.

The 2001 season had another weather anomaly with a hurricane postponing the Florida State game until December 1. But the season was also O'Leary's last, as he was sought by Notre Dame to take over for the departing Bob Davie. Mac McWhorter took over before the Seattle Bowl loss to Stanford as the team lost three of their last four. O'Leary ended up having to resign from his new job in South Bend after the school realized that the coach had lied on his resume about both his academic and athletic backgrounds.

Tech athletic director Dave Braine brought Americus native Chan Gailey to succeed O'Leary and McWhorter. Gailey had the pedigree, coming from a background of successful coordinating and head coaching positions in the colleges and the pros (Samford, Troy and the Dallas Cowboys), but his era could be characterized by being just okay, not threatening for the ACC Championship for most of his tenure and never beating Georgia in his six seasons. The won-lost records were more fit for tennis matches than titles: 7-6 in 2002; 7-5 in 2003 as eleven players were declared academically ineligible (Gailey started a freshman at quarterback in Reggie Ball); 7-5 in 2004; and 7-5 in 2005, even with a preseason top-twenty ranking and losing three of the Jackets' last four.

The year 2005 also brought more undue attention to campus involving Reuben Houston, his problems with the law, his subsequent reinstatement and the resolution of the NCAA investigation involving more issues with the initially ineligible players from 2003. The end result was probation, scholarship reductions and the eventual retirement of Athletic Director Dave Braine. Dan Radakovich took over.

The year 2006 was the one Tech fans were looking for when Gailey was brought to the Flats. With quarterback Reggie Ball throwing as much as possible to wide receiver Calvin Johnson, a season-opening loss to Notre Dame didn't faze the squad. The team won five in a row to get to 9-2, but the late-season fade happened again with three straight losses even as the Jackets won the Coastal Division Championship. All were by three points: Georgia, 15–12; Wake, 9–6, in an ACC title game that pundits claimed set the sport back years; and West Virginia, 38–35, in the Gator Bowl. Patience in Gailey was wearing thin as he headed into 2007.

Gailey didn't make it through the year. The defending division champs went 7-6, lost to Georgia for the sixth time under Gailey and were coached by defensive coordinator Jon Tenuta in a Humanitarian Bowl loss to Fresno State.

Paul Johnson's offense brings fits to the ACC. *Georgia Tech Athletic Association.*

The athletic department had to do something to restore the faith and went to Navy to get its man, Paul Johnson. Johnson's offense had been unstoppable at Georgia Southern and unstoppable at the Naval Academy, restoring its program to national on-field prominence, so Dan Radakovich brought Johnson's flexbone/wishbone/option offense to Grant Field. Some college football fans thought that Johnson's success was a gimmick that couldn't work in "major college football." Others thought that because it was so radically different from the conventional, pro-style, cookie-cutter offense that was trending heavily in the modern day, it just might work.

Johnson proved the naysayers wrong with a 9-4 season during which the marquee wins included Florida State (for the first time ever in Tallahassee), Virginia Tech and Georgia before losing to LSU in the Peach Bowl. His tenacious defense and Greene County–grad quarterback Joshua Nesbitt followed that season up with an 11-3, top fifteen ranking (ranked as high as seventh before losing to UGA) and a win over Clemson in the ACC Championship game—one eventually vacated after future

NCAA infractions would be disclosed. Even a loss to Iowa in the Orange Bowl continued the optimism with a "gimmick" offense in a senior-laden squad. Johnson was named ACC Coach of the Year.

The last two seasons have been rebuilding years for Johnson and Tech as they went 6-7 and 8-5, but Johnson has proven once again that certain athletes placed in certain systems can succeed and bring wins in different ways to college football for a program that has to do things differently because of its academic standards.

Shorter Begins

What happens when you have to start from scratch? Shorter College (now University) in Rome brought on renowned college and high school coach Phil Jones to build an NAIA program that started in 2002—but without footballs, football equipment, practice fields, staff, offices or players. One condition put forth by the NAIA meant the Hawks' program had to be built with twenty-four scholarships for one hundred players, but the biggest condition was that the school had to play a varsity schedule from the beginning. Coach Jones had no idea what to do next, but he had an idea that early damage could last a long time.

"I began to pray as I knew that I had no real human answer that was sufficient. While praying, I kept hearing the word 'relationships,'" Jones admits. "I knew that God was communicating to me that 'relationships' would be our 'foundation.' We began to study the word 'relationships' and concluded that Max Lucado was right on when he stated that 'nothing motivates us any more than a relationship.'"

That first season with freshmen went 3-7, but Jones and his staff kept plugging along. The freshmen turned into sophomores, and the wins came more often than the losses. Back-to-back seasons of 7-4 set up the senior season for those original two dozen players who had been around since the beginning.

"In a spiritual sense, I knew that the number one relationship in my life was my relationship with Jesus Christ, and that relationship could not be destroyed by a scoreboard. Then we began to talk to recruits and their families about relationships and share our relationship with Him," Jones added. "We did not tell them that they had to go to a certain church or

AJ Cooley. *Shorter University Sports Information Department.*

even know about Christ as they came, but that we were going to share our faith with them. It began to grow."

The 2008 season was captained by tailback A.J. Cooley and linebacker Logan Lollis. A win on the road in McKenzie, Tennessee, against Bethel University gave the Hawks a share of the Western Division title in the Mid-South Conference and their first playoff bid against Cumberlands (Kentucky). "We then talked to our players about relationships in family that are so important, realizing that those relationships were incredible motivation for each one of us in a family. We then talked to them about relationships on a football team. We tried to express to them that when they are in a huddle with ten other guys, the way you feel about those other ten and the way they feel about you has an incredible impact on how hard you will play when the ball is snapped."

Close to thirty seniors were recognized after the season ended in the first round of the NAIA playoffs. The program continues on-the-field successes, but more important for Coach Jones and his staff is making sure that those relationships he talks about continue off the field long after their players have stopped drilling, tackling and scoring.

We wanted to emphasize that businesses with employees who understand relationships with each other are probably those businesses who overcome difficulty in a down time, as do families who respond to the relationships in the family. Beginning with player-to-player relationships, family relationships and our relationship with God, through Christ, we had a foundation that was a great motivation and a great foundation to begin and that could grow. We believe that God intended it that way, in the beginning, in that Adam and Eve had a personal relationship with God as they walked with Him in the garden daily until there was sin. Then God chose not to destroy us because of sin but to send His only Son, who knew no sin, to die for us rather than God deciding to just do away with human beings due to our sin. All of us have sinned.

The program experienced its first losing season two years ago as relationships continued to build not only on the field but off it as well. The team rebounded with a season above .500 in 2011. But the challenges are coming from different places as the Hawks move forward.

AS DOES GEORGIA STATE

In November 2006, Georgia State University commissioned a feasibility study of its own for football. Former Atlanta Falcons head coach Dan Reeves was hired as a consultant to look into starting a program five months later.

A year later, Bill Curry was named coach of another Atlanta-based football program and became the first head coach for the Panthers on April 17, 2008. The school was preparing for a 2010 debut on the field, but the Colonial Athletic Association decided in June 2009 that it would accept GSU in time for the 2012 season.

On September 2, 2010, Georgia State played its first football game in front of a crowd of 30,237 at the Georgia Dome and beat Shorter, 41–7. Parris Lee went into the Panthers record books with the first touchdown, a four-yard run.

"I've never been more proud of a group of young men than I am of this group," Curry said after the game. After starting out the season 1-2, Curry's team ripped off a four-game win streak against Campbell, Morehead State, Savannah State and NC Central. A win against Lamar guaranteed a winning

Georgia State's first-ever kickoff. *Georgia State University Sports Information Department.*

season in the first year, but the season ended in Tuscaloosa, Alabama, against the Crimson Tide.

"I told them before the game, I'm going to be proud of you regardless of the outcome, and I am," said Curry after losing, 63–7, to finish 6-5. "We're a better football team right now than we were before the game because of what we learned. I'm grateful to our administration for making this happen, and I'm grateful to Alabama."

The 2011 season finished 3-8 as Georgia State prepared for its introduction into the Colonial, but its introduction would be a short one.

THE END OF MBC AND MGC

Morris Brown College, the only college in Georgia founded by African Americans, lost an appeal to keep its accreditation in April 2003. The school suspended its athletics programs—the first NCAA Division I school to disband all sports at once as part of being $27 million in debt.

"We've shut down the program, but there is no decision beyond another year," Athletic Director Russell Ellington said at the time. "I'm assuming that we won't have an athletics program again until further notice."

Fourteen sports were dissolved, all of the coaches were instantly laid off and the sports never returned. Morris Brown lost its accreditation in December 2002 because of a lack of financial stability. It had decided to pursue a Division I program in 2000 in an attempt to bolster its reputation and become more viable in the marketplace. The basketball program turned into barnstormers, playing only a handful of games at home and grabbing a paycheck wherever they could. And after only one year, the school still operated under a $1.6 million department deficit. Football was no different. In mid-January 2003, then head football coach Sol Brannan told the *Atlanta Journal-Constitution* that he had spent "close to $40,000" of his own money on recruiting just before Brannan and his staff were fired.

Middle Georgia College, originally the Twelfth District Agricultural and Mechanical School, also fell victim to shrinking budgets, twice. Starting for the first time in 1923, the Wolverines programs won junior college conference titles in 1930, 1931 and 1933 under John T. "Jake" Morris. In 1934, Jake Morris's team won the Southern States Championship, beating a Wally Butts–coached Georgia Military College in Milledgeville. Names like Jody Matt, Cliff Goggins and Joe Glisson would be remembered for their part in the school's history. Glisson scored on an eighty-one-yard touchdown to knock off the rival South Georgia squad coached by Bobby Bowden. The school suspended football after the 1960 season.

In October 1993, the board of regents gave permission for Middle Georgia to bring the sport back, with Dennis Roland as head coach. But after nine seasons, then interim president Robert Watts suspended the program again because of growing debts and told the assembled media, "The athletic program has a multiyear debt that's been carried forward of about $73,000, and I'm running close to somewhere around $90,000 in debt for the current year, so that's about $160,000 just in the athletic department, and we have to find a way to get out of that and not just that temporary, one-time debt."

Garrett Hagin, the Warriors' first-year head coach, had no idea. "I wish they would have let me know so I could've discussed my concerns," Hagin said.

So, football died in the town of Cochran not once but twice, even if, as some say, a few MGC alums wanted to step up and handle the cost of the entire athletic program. They were turned down flat.

But the school will have its place in college football history. In January 1999, Tonya Butler signed a national letter of intent for a football scholarship to compete as placekicker for Head Coach Randy Pippin, making her the first woman to earn a football scholarship at a state school. During her two years at Middle Georgia, Butler made thirty-six of forty-two extra points and one field goal for the Warriors. Butler earned her associate degree at Middle Georgia but ended up going to Georgia Southern to play soccer, graduating in 2003.

Pippin contacted Butler and got her to be his place kicker at the University of West Alabama as a grad student in 2003 and 2004. In the first game of the 2003 season, she kicked a field goal against Stillman and was recognized as the first woman to kick a field goal in a college football game.

THE FUTURE

The landscape for the sport is always changing, and in the state of Georgia, the game will be different as we move forward to add more history to where we are. Fifteen schools have active programs heading into the 2012 season, with two adding the game in the near future and four more schools looking at the prospects of having the sport on campus.

Here's what we have to look forward to. The University of Georgia will move into the future without one of its most polarizing figures, President Michael Adams. He plans to step down after the upcoming 2012–13 academic year. Adams has been president since 1997, when he succeeded Charles Knapp. The university has been consistently ranked as one of the nation's top public universities and has had enrollment grow by six thousand to thirty-five thousand. The school secured close to $1 billion for capital improvements during his tenure and raised millions in endowments and scholarships.

"We're a better university because of Dr. Adams," said Jerry Daniel, president of the UGA Staff Council in an interview with the *Atlanta Journal-Constitution*. "He's always been a fighter for us. Whoever comes after him will have big shoes to fill."

They'll also have a replacement for UGA VIII "Big Bad Bruce." According to Sonny Seiler, the keeper of the Bulldog mascot breeding and training program and owner of the Damn Good Dawgs, he has two or three contenders for the title of UGA IX. He plans on making an announcement at Picture Day and will have the passing of the collar at the first game of the season.

But the mascot tradition also lost one of its own in late March 2012 as Marie Coleman Wilson passed at the age of eighty-six. Mrs. Wilson made sure that her family's sour mug English Bulldog, Mr. Angel, would be included in the line of official mascots the school recognizes as part of its heritage.

Uga, as we know him now, started when second-year law student Sonny took his bulldog puppy to the Florida State game in 1956. Then sports information director Dan Magill first noticed the puppy and brought a picture to then coach Wally Butts. But there was a gap in time between the original goat in 1892, Trilby the bull terrier in 1894 and the dogs "Butch," "Tuffy" and "Mike" that were around campus from 1947 to 1955.

That's where Mrs. Wilson comes into the history. She was a student in 1944–46 and had Mr. Angel around campus. Wilson provided the *Red and Black* newspaper with photographs of Mr. Angel at football games and with cheerleaders, and he was even pictured on the field during the 1944 and 1945 homecomings in *Pandora* yearbooks.

Wilson's unwavering efforts to have Mr. Angel in the lineage were officially recognized in 2008 after years of contacting the university and even enlisting the aid of Loran Smith and, later, Seiler himself. He was officially recognized in the *Red and Black*, in the 2008 football media guide, in newspaper articles around the state, in a special announcement to the crowd in Sanford Stadium and in a special dedication ceremony in his hometown of Eastman, Georgia. When he passed, he was buried under his favorite cherry laurel trees in his backyard—now the location of the Bank of Eastman. A bronze statue of Mr. Angel was created in his honor by master sculptor Victor Worth, and you can still see it in Dodge County today. Had it not been for Wilson's tireless efforts, only part of the Bulldog mascot history would be known.

Georgia State is moving to the Sun Belt Conference after one season in the Colonial Athletic Association in Division I-AA. "Under President Becker's leadership, Georgia State University is growing in size and stature as one of the nation's leading urban research institutions, so it is only fitting that our athletic program moves to the top level of college athletics," said GSU director of Athletics Cheryl Levick at the presser where they were welcomed by Sun Belt commissioner Karl Benson.

GSU selects Bill Curry to build its program. *Georgia State University Sports Information Department.*

"We want to thank Chancellor Hawkins and Commissioner Benson for this opportunity, and we look forward to an exciting new era in Georgia State Athletics. The Sun Belt Conference is a tremendous fit for Georgia State, offering top-quality competition, increased exposure and the chance to build rivalries with schools in driving distance for our fans."

Georgia Southern president Brooks Keel told the *Statesboro Herald* newspaper that the school is looking to raise more than $36 million over the next eight years for a move to Division I (or FBS). The funds are for an increase in the seating at Paulson Stadium and construction of a new football field house. "There's no question it's where we want to go," Keel said.

Shorter University is leaving the NAIA and is heading to the Gulf South Conference and NCAA Division II. "The Gulf South Conference is one of the premier conferences in NCAA Division II, and we are very proud that they endorsed us for NCAA Division II membership," said Shorter University athletic director Bill Peterson when the Hawks were endorsed for membership. "We look forward to beginning competition within the GSC in 2012–13 and beginning competitive rivalries

Above: Shorter University is heading to NCAA Division II. *Shorter University Sports Information Department.*

Left: Bobby Lamb restarts Mercer football. *Mercer University Sports Information Department.*

with folks such as Valdosta State, West Georgia, North Alabama, the University of Alabama–Huntsville and all of the other great schools in that conference."

Head Coach Phil Jones is looking forward to this new set of challenges, rivalries and relationships as well, with his new student-athletes for NCAA play and the ones who are coming with him from the NAIA: "The relationships we have enable us to give of ourselves for something larger than ourselves. Is that not what the best families do and what the best businesses do in troubled times? People inside the business understand that I am willing to give of myself for something larger than myself. That's what great teams do as well. If it is not a great team, it becomes a better team than the talent suggests it would."

While some schools are moving, some are adding the sport. Mercer University is bringing back the Bears after a seventy-three-year absence for play to start in 2013. An on-campus football stadium and facility is being constructed, and Bobby Lamb was named the school's first head coach. The Bears will play in the Pioneer Football League, debuting at the same time as Stetson University's rebirth.

"I have been very impressed with President Underwood and Athletic Director Jim Cole and the vision and leadership they are providing at Mercer," Lamb said when he was hired.

> One of the qualities that most attracted me to Mercer was their emphasis on the true student-athlete. I have spent the past twenty-nine years at an institution with very similar expectations.
>
> Sometimes the term "student-athlete" is used nonchalantly. People forget that it is "student" first and "athlete" second. I have always stressed the importance of academics before athletics as a player, coach and father. I believe my philosophy for building strong men who will become leaders in their communities will be a perfect fit with Mercer.

Reinhardt University is entering the NAIA, and it is bringing one of the state's most respected high school coaches to lead the Eagles into play, Danny Cronic. "I'm really excited about the opportunity," he said in an interview with the *Newnan Times-Herald*'s Tommy Camp. "I've wanted to coach on the college level for a long time and I'm just elated. I can't tell you how happy I am. It's like I've gotten a new burst of energy. I don't remember being as happy about a job as I am with this one. I guess the Lord just blessed the old war horse one more time."

"Dr. Cronic's experience and his record of success will translate into winning Reinhardt football," said Reinhardt president Dr. J. Thomas Isherwood when the announcement was made. "It is very important for our coaches to share our institution's values and to demonstrate that they can work effectively with young people to build character. We have succeeded in meeting all these goals with Dr. Danny Cronic. His hiring marks a very important step forward for this dynamic new program."

Cronic was a high school coach in the area near Reinhardt's Waleska home forty years ago—even rooming with the mayor of the town back then. Cronic's Eagles are anticipating 70 players in year one and 110 in year two. "They wanted someone with experience, someone with maturity," he said. "I guess I'm covered up with maturity."

And, finally, while Point University starts its first year of NAIA competition, Kennesaw State University, Brewton-Parker College, Truett-McConnell College and Augusta's Paine College are all thinking about it. Kennesaw plans to start in the FCS in 2014, playing at its soccer stadium. The school enlisted Vince Dooley as part of its exploratory committee, but in announcing the school's plans, he mistakenly referred to his location as "Kansas State" before the student body attending the press conference reminded him where he was.

School president Daniel Papp said that having football will "increase and expand national recognition of the institution, highlight important work taking place on campus in teaching, research, scholarship, creative activities and service."

Brewton-Parker approved a football feasibility study in the fall of 2009 to see if the school would be interested in adding football back to its on-campus sports. In the last year, BPC president Dr. Mike Simoneaux even admitted in television interviews that he would like to pursue the idea further. Truett-McConnell College in Cleveland is also looking into the idea of adding football to its list of sports, as is Paine College in Augusta.

WRDW-TV's Kevin Faigle caught up with Athletic Director Tim Duncan in January 2012 to see if the Augusta-based school would be interested in reviving a sport that ceased on campus in the early 1960s.

"Division II and liberal arts schools like Paine College are driven so much by enrollment that an additional eighty to one hundred young men coming to Paine College to play football would be attractive for us because we're 65 percent women, and that could change the dynamics of our student population for the good," Duncan said about a team on the Division II level.

"That's part of the study itself," added Duncan. "How we would lay out the initial start-up cost and how we would fund it annually. Annual costs we could definitely take care of because of the increased enrollment. We're still investigating the initial cost."

The history written and read here, then, is a big beginning for a future.

ALL THE WINS AND LOSSES
WE COULD FIND

UNIVERSITY OF GEORGIA

Head Coach	Year(s)	Record
Dr. Charles Herty	1892	1-1-0
Ernest Brown	1893	2-2-1
Robert Winston	1894	5-1-0
Glenn Warner (2 years, 7-4-0)	1895	3-4-0
	1896	4-0-0
Charles McCarthy (2 years, 6-3-0)	1897	2-1-0
	1898	4-2-0
Gordon Saussy	1899	2-3-1

Head Coach	Year(s)	Record
E.E. Jones	1900	2-4-0
Billy Reynolds (2 years, 5-7-3)	1901	1-5-2
	1902	4-2-1
M.M. Dickinson	1903	3-4-0
Charles A. Barnard	1904	1-5-0
M.M. Dickinson	1905	1-5-0
W.S. Whitney (2 years, 6-7-2)	1906	2-4-1
	1907	4-3-1
Branch Bocock	1908	5-2-1
J. Coulter	1909	1-4-2
W.A. Cunningham (8 years, 43-18-9)	1910	6-2-1
	1911	7-1-1
	1912	6-1-1
	1913	6-2-0
	1914	3-5-1
	1915	5-2-2
	1916	6-3-0
	1917–1918	no games
	1919	4-2-3
H.J. Stegeman (3 years, 20-6-3)	1920	8-0-1 (SIAA Champions)
	1921	7-2-1
	1922	5-4-1
George Woodruff (5 years, 30-16-1)	1923	5-3-1
	1924	7-3-0

Head Coach	Year(s)	Record
	1925	4-5-0
	1926	5-4-0
	1927	9-1-0 (National Champions)
Harry Mehre (10 years, 59-34-6)	1928	4-5-0
	1929	6-4-0
	1930	7-2-1
	1931	8-2-0
	1932	2-5-2
	1933	8-2-0
	1934	7-3-0
	1935	6-4-0
	1936	5-4-1
	1937	6-3-2
Joel Hunt	1938	5-4-1
Wally Butts (22 years, 140-86-9)	1939	5-6-0
	1940	5-4-1
	1941	9-1-1
	1942	11-1-0 (National/SEC Champions)
	1943	6-4-0
	1944	7-3-0
	1945	9-2-0
	1946	11-0-0 (National/SEC Champions)
	1947	7-4-1

Head Coach	Year(s)	Record
	1948	9-2-0 (SEC Champions)
	1949	4-6-1
	1950	6-3-3
	1951	5-5-0
	1952	7-4-0
	1953	3-8-0
	1954	6-3-1
	1955	4-6-0
	1956	3-6-1
	1957	3-7-0
	1958	4-6-0
	1959	10-1-0 (SEC Champions)
	1960	6-4-0
Johnny Griffith (3 years, 10-16-4)	1961	3-7-0
	1962	3-4-3
	1963	4-5-1
Vince Dooley (25 years, 201-77-10)	1964	7-3-1
	1965	6-4-0
	1966	10-1-0 (SEC Champions)
	1967	7-4-0
	1968	8-1-2 (National/SEC Champions)
	1969	5-5-1
	1970	5-5-0

Terry Hoage. *Georgia Athletic Association.*

Head Coach	Year(s)	Record
	1971	11-1-0
	1972	7-4-0
	1973	7-4-1
	1974	6-6-0
	1975	9-3-0
	1976	10-2-0 (SEC Champions)
	1977	5-6-0
	1978	9-2-1
	1979	6-5-0

Head Coach	Year(s)	Record
	1980	12-0-0 (National/SEC Champions)
	1981	10-2-0 (SEC Champions)
	1982	11-1-0 (SEC Champions)
	1983	10-1-1
	1984	7-4-1
	1985	7-3-2
	1986	8-4-0
	1987	9-3-0
	1988	9-3-0
Ray Goff (7 years, 46-34-1)	1989	6-6-0
	1990	4-7-0
	1991	9-3-0
	1992	10-2-0
	1993	5-6-0
	1994	6-4-1
	1995	6-6-0
Jim Donnan (5 years, 40-19-0)	1996	5-6-0
	1997	10-2-0
	1998	9-3-0
	1999	8-4-0
	2000	8-4-0
Mark Richt (11 years, 106-38-0)	2001	8-4-0

Head Coach	Year(s)	Record
	2002	13-1-0 (SEC Champions)
	2003	11-3-0 (SEC Eastern Champions)
	2004	10-2-0
	2005	10-3-0 (SEC Champions)
	2006	9-4-0
	2007	11-2-0
	2008	10-3-0
	2009	8-5-0
	2010	6-7-0
	2011	10-4-0

GEORGIA TECH

Head Coach	Year(s)	Record
E.E. West	1892	0-3-0
Frank Spain/Lt. Leonard Wood	1893	2-1-1
	1894	0-3-0
	1895	no team
	1896	1-1-1
	1897	0-1-0
R.B. Nalley	1898	0-3-0
Mr. Collier	1899	0-5-0
	1900	0-4-0

Grant Field, circa 1912. *Georgia Tech Athletic Association.*

Head Coach	Year(s)	Record
Dr. Cyrus Strickler	1901	4-0-1
John McKee	1902	0-6-2
Jesse Thrash	1903	2-5-0
John Heisman (16 years, 102-29-7)	1904	8-1-1
	1905	6-0-1
	1906	5-3-1
	1907	4-4-0
	1908	6-3-0
	1909	7-2-0
	1910	5-3-0

Head Coach	Year(s)	Record
	1911	6-2-1
	1912	5-3-1
	1913	7-2-0
	1914	6-2-0
	1915	7-0-1
	1916	8-0-1 (SIAA Champions)
	1917	9-0-0 (SIAA/National Champions)
	1918	6-1-0 (SIAA Co-Champions)
	1919	7-3-0
William Alexander (25 years, 134-95-15)	1920	8-1-0 (SIAA Co-Champions)
	1921	8-1-0 (SIAA Co-Champions/ Southern Conference)
	1922	7-2-0 (Southern Conference Co-Champions)
	1923	3-2-4
	1924	5-3-1
	1925	6-2-1
	1926	4-5-0
	1927	8-1-1 (Southern Conference Co-Champions)
	1928	10-0 (Rose Bowl win/Southern Conference/Co-National Champions)

Head Coach	Year(s)	Record
	1929	3-6-0
	1930	2-6-1
	1931	2-7-1
	1932	4-5-1 (SEC)
	1933	5-5-0
	1934	1-9-0
	1935	5-5-0
	1936	5-5-1
	1937	6-3-1
	1938	3-4-3
	1939	8-2-0 (SEC Co-Champions)
	1940	3-7-0
	1941	3-6-0
	1942	9-2-0
	1943	8-3-0 (SEC Champions)
	1944	8-3-0 (SEC Champions)
Bobby Dodd (22 years, 165-64-8)	1945	4-6-0
	1946	9-2-0
	1947	10-1-0
	1948	7-3-0
	1949	7-3-0
	1950	5-6-0
	1951	11-0-1 (SEC Champions)

Head Coach	Year(s)	Record
	1952	12-0-0 (SEC/Co-National Champions)
	1953	9-2-1
	1954	8-3-0
	1955	9-1-1
	1956	10-1-0
	1957	4-4-2
	1958	5-4-1
	1959	6-5-0
	1960	5-5-0
	1961	7-4-0
	1962	7-3-1
	1963	7-3-0 (Independent)
	1964	7-3-0
	1965	7-3-1
	1966	9-2-0
Bud Carson (5 years, 27-27)	1967	4-6-0
	1968	4-6-0
	1969	4-6-0
	1970	9-3-0
	1971	6-6-0
Bill Fulcher (2 years, 12-10-1)	1972	7-4-1
	1973	5-6-0
Pepper Rodgers (6 years, 34-31-2)	1974	6-5-0

Head Coach	Year(s)	Record
	1975	7-4-0
	1976	4-6-1
	1977	6-5-0
	1978	7-5-0 (Atlantic Coast Conference)
	1979	4-6-1
Bill Curry (7 years, 31-43-4)	1980	1-9-1
	1981	1-10-0
	1982	6-5-0
	1983	3-8-0
	1984	6-4-1
	1985	9-2-1
	1986	5-5-1
Bobby Ross (5 years, 31-26-1)	1987	2-9-0
	1988	3-8-0
	1989	7-4-0
	1990	11-0-1 (ACC/National Champions)
	1991	8-5-0
Bill Lewis (3 years, 11-19)	1992	5-6-0
	1993	5-6-0
	1994	1-10-0
George O'Leary (7 years, 52-33)	1995	6-5-0
	1996	5-6-0
	1997	7-5-0

Head Coach	Year(s)	Record
	1998	10-2-0 (ACC Co-Champions)
	1999	8-4-0
	2000	9-3-0
	2001	8-5-0
Chan Gailey (6 years, 44-32)	2002	7-6-0
	2003	7-6-0
	2004	7-5 0
	2005	7-5-0
	2006	9-5-0
	2007	7-6-0
Paul Johnson (4 years, 25-14)	2008	9-4-0
	2009	11-3-0 (ACC Champions)
	2010	6-7-0
	2011	8-5-0

GEORGIA SOUTHERN

GEORGIA NORMAL SCHOOL

Head Coach	Year(s)	Record
E.G. Cromartie (3 years, 7-5-1)	1924	1-0-0
	1925	1-2-0
	1926	5-3-1

Paulsen Stadium. *Georgia Southern University Sports Information Department.*

Head Coach	Year(s)	Record
H.A. Woodle (2 years, 11-6-1)	1927	6-1-1
	1928	5-5-0

SOUTH GEORGIA TEACHERS COLLEGE

B.L. "Crook" Smith (13 years, 45-67-7)	1929	2-1-2
	1930	3-3-2
	1931	3-6-0
	1932	7-3-0
	1933	5-4-0
	1934	5-6-0
	1935	3-3-2

Head Coach	Year(s)	Record
	1936	2-9-0
	1937	2-9-0
	1938	3-5-1

GEORGIA TEACHERS COLLEGE

	1939	5-5-0
	1940	3-5-0
	1941	2-8-0

GEORGIA SOUTHERN COLLEGE

Erk Russell (8 years, 83-22-1)	1982	7-3-1
	1983	6-5-0
	1984	8-3-0
	1985	13-2-0 (National Champions)
	1986	13-2-0 (National Champions)
	1987	9-4-0
	1988	12-3-0 (National Runners-Up)
	1989	15-0-0 (National Champions)

GEORGIA SOUTHERN UNIVERSITY

Head Coach	Year(s)	Record
Tim Stowers (8 years, 83-22-1)	1990	12-3-0 (National Champions)
	1991	7-4-0
	1992	7-4-0
	1993	10-3-0
	1994	6-5-0
	1995	9-4-0 (National Quarterfinalists)
Frank Ellwood	1996	4-7-0
Paul Johnson (5 years, 62-10)	1997	10-3-0 (National Quarterfinalists/Southern Conference Champions)
	1998	14-1-0 (National Runners-Up/Southern Conference Champions)
	1999	13-2-0 (National Champions/Southern Conference Champions)
	2000	13-2-0 (National Champions/Southern Conference Champions)
	2001	12-2-0 (National Semifinalists/Southern Conference Champions)

Head Coach	Year(s)	Record
Mike Sewak (4 years, 35-14)	2002	11-3-0 (National Semifinalists/ Southern Conference Champions)
	2003	7-4-0
	2004	9-3-0 (Southern Conference Champions)
	2005	8-4-0
Brian VanGorder	2006	3-8-0
Chris Hatcher (3 years, 18-15)	2007	7-4-0
	2008	6-5-0
	2009	5-6-0
Jeff Monken (2 years, 21-8)	2010	10-5-0 (National Semifinalists)
	2011	11-3-0 (National Semifinalists/ Southern Conference Champions)

GEORGIA STATE UNIVERSITY

Head Coach	Year(s)	Record
Bill Curry	2010	6-5-0
	2011	3-8-0

WEST GEORGIA

Head Coach	Year(s)	Record
Ken Johnson	1957	0-8-0
Dick Ottinger	1958	0-6-0
Bobby Pate (4 years, 28-15)	1981	9-1-0
	1982	12-0-0 (National Champions)
	1983	4-6-0
	1984	3-8-0
Frank Vohun (4 years, 15-26)	1985	5-5-0
	1986	4-6-0
	1987	2-9-0
	1988	4-6-0
Mac McWhorter	1989	4-7-0
Ron Jurney (3 years, 12-21)	1990	1-10-0
	1991	6-5-0
	1992	5-6-0
Charlie Fisher (5 years, 36-17)	1993	4-6-0
	1994	7-3-0
	1995	8-3-0
	1996	9-3-0
	1997	8-2-0
Glenn Spencer (3 years, 28-7)	1998	10-2-0
	1999	8-3-0
	2000	10-2-0

West Georgia's 1982 title. *University of West Georgia Sports Information Department.*

Head Coach	Year(s)	Record
Gary Otten	2001	8-3-0
Mike Ledford (6 years, 18-45)	2002	3-8-0
	2003	3-8-0
	2004	2-7-0
	2005	7-4-0
	2006	1-9-0
	2007	2-9-0
Daryl Dickey (4 years, 10-30)	2008	0-10-0
	2009	1-9-0
	2010	3-7-0
	2011	6-4-0

VALDOSTA STATE

Head Coach	Year(s)	Record
Jim Goodman (4 years, 20-23-1)	1982	5-5-1
	1983	5-6-0
	1984	5-6-0
	1985	5-6-0
Jim Berryman	1986	9-2-0
Mike Cavan (5 years, 28-20-2)	1987	6-4-0
	1988	6-3-1
	1989	5-5-0
	1990	5-5-0
	1991	6-3-1
Hal Mumme (5 years, 46-22-1)	1992	5-4-1
	1993	8-3-0
	1994	11-2-0
	1995	6-5-0
	1996	10-3-0
Mike Kelly (3 years, 15-16)	1997	6-5-0
	1998	5-6-0
	1999	4-5-0
Mark Nelson (interim)		
Chris Hatcher (7 years, 76-11)	2000	10-2-0
	2001	12-1-0

Head Coach	Year(s)	Record
	2002	14-1-0 (National Runners-Up)
	2003	10-2-0
	2004	13-1-0 (National Champions)
	2005	9-3-0
	2006	8-2-0
David Dean (5 years, 42-15)	2007	13-1-0 (National Champions)
	2008	9-3-0
	2009	6-4-0
	2010	8-3-0
	2011	6-4-0

ALBANY STATE COLLEGE/UNIVERSITY

Head Coach	Year(s)	Record
Hampton Smith (4 years, 22-19)	1993	11-1-0
	1994	10-2-0
	1995	8-4-0
	1996	8-3-0
	1997	11-1-0 (Division II, Quarterfinal)
	1998	3-2-0

Head Coach	Year(s)	Record
	1999	7-3-0
	2000	4-6-0
	2001	4-6-0
	2002	7-4-0
Mike White (9 years, 78-24)	2003	10-2-0
	2004	11-1-0 (Division II, Quarterfinal)
	2005	8-2-0
	2006	7-4-0
	2007	8-3-0
	2008	7-4-0
	2009	8-3-0
	2010	11-1-0 (Division II, Quarterfinal)
	2011	8-4-0

MOREHOUSE COLLEGE

Head Coach	Year(s)	Record
Charles Willis	1900–1901	0-2-0
A.D. "Doc" Jones	1902–4	2-2-2
Samuel "Big Boy" Archer (co-coach)	1905–8, 1912–15	35-2-5
Matthew Bullock (co-coach)	1910	4-1-0
	1911	4-1-0

162

The 1950 Morehouse squad. *Morehouse College Sports Information Department.*

Head Coach	Year(s)	Record
	1912	5-0-0
	1913	3-1-2
	1914	5-1-0
	1915	2-0-2
Burwell T. Harvey (10 years, 49-13-4)	1916	6-0-0
	1917	3-1-0
	1918	1-2-0
	1919	6-1-0
	1920	5-1-0
	1921	7-0-0
	1922	5-2-0
	1923	6-2-1
	1924	5-3-1
	1925	5-1-2

"Red" Smith's 1943 Morehouse College Maroon Tigers. *Morehouse Sports Information Department.*

Head Coach	Year(s)	Record
Ted Robinson	1926	2-5-1
Burwell T. Harvey (2 years, 8-10-2)	1927	5-5-1
	1928	3-5-1
Ray Vaughn (3 years, 15-10-1)	1929	4-4-0
	1930	9-1-0
	1931	2-5-1
Franklin L. Robinson (2 years, 7-7-2)	1932	3-4-1
	1933	4-3-1

Head Coach	Year(s)	Record
J. Mayo "Ink" Williams	1934	4-3-2
Franklin L. Robinson (8 years, 26-28-8)	1935	5-1-1
	1936	4-2-2
	1937	2-3-2
	1938	4-3-1
	1939	4-3-1
	1940	1-6-1
	1941	3-5-0
	1942	3-5-0
Vernon "Red" Smith (2 years, 5-6-1)	1943	2-2-1
	1944	3-4-0
Franklin L. Robinson (5 years, 12-22-4)	1945	1-5-0
	1946	1-4-3
	1947	3-5-0
	1948	4-4-0
	1949	3-4-1
Joseph Echols (5 years, 16-22-2)	1950	1-6-1
	1951	3-4-0
	1952	3-5-1
	1953	5-3-0
	1954	4-4-0
James E. "Pinky" Haines (2 years, 4-10-2)	1955	3-3-2
	1956	1-7-0

Head Coach	Year(s)	Record
Duke Foster Jr. (10 years, 27-47-4)	1957	2-5-1
	1958	3-4-1
	1959	5-2-1
	1960	5-3-0
	1961	4-4-0
	1962	6-2-0
	1963	1-6-0
	1964	1-7-0
	1965	0-6-1
	1966	0-8-0
Henry "Hank" Darlington (5 years, 17-24-2)	1967	3-6-0
	1968	3-3-2
	1969	4-5-0
	1970	3-6-0
	1971	4-4-0
Frank Merchant	1972	6-2-0
Michael Gray (6 years, 18-34-1)	1973	4-3-1
	1974	2-7-0
	1975	0-9-0
	1976	4-5-0
	1977	4-5-0
	1978	4-5-0
Maurice "Mo" Hunt (11 years, 48-57-3)	1979	6-3-0
	1980	3-6-0
	1981	4-6-0

Head Coach	Year(s)	Record
	1982	5-5-0
	1983	6-4-0
	1984	5-4-1
	1985	3-6-1
	1986	5-5-0
	1987	5-5-0
	1988	4-7-0
	1989	2-6-1
Dwight Scales	1990	1-7-1
Craig M. Cason (3 years, 17-14)	1991	6-4-0
	1992	6-5-0
	1993	5-5-0
Vincent "Chico" Williams	1994	3-7-0
Maurice "Mo" Hunt (2 years, 7-15)	1995	5-6-0
	1996	2-9-0
Douglass Williams	1997	3-8-0
Frank Hickson	1998	0-11-0
Anthony Jones (3 years, 18-13)	1999	2-8-0
	2000	8-3-0
	2001	8-2-0
Willard Scissum (3 years, 14-18)	2002	6-5-0
	2003	4-7-0
	2004	4-6-0
Terry Buford (2 years, 7-14)	2005	4-6-0

Morehouse eyes a return to the Division II playoffs. *Morehouse Sports Information Department.*

Head Coach	Year(s)	Record
	2006	3-8-0
Rich Freeman (5 years, 36-15)	2007	7-3-0
	2008	6-4-0
	2009	7-3-0
	2010	8-3-0
	2011	8-2-0
Total	**1900– present**	**431-441-48**

FORT VALLEY STATE

Head Coach	Year(s)	Record
Richard Craig (9 years, 40-30-3)	1945	1-0-0
	1946	0-8-0
	1947	7-0-1
	1948	7-1-0
	1949	5-3-1
	1950	7-3-0
	1951	1-8-0
	1952	5-4-1
	1953	7-3-0
Ousley Gates (2 years, 8-9)	1954	5-3-0
	1955	3-6-0
Alva Tabor Jr. (4 years, 18-13-3)	1956	2-5-1
	1957	6-3-0
	1958	5-2-1
	1959	5-3-1
Alphonso Varner	1960	1-5-3
James Hawkins	1961	0-9-0
Alphonso Varner	1962	2-7-0
Leon Lomax (14 years, 87-33-7)	1963	3-6-0
	1964	7-2-0
	1965	5-2-1

Head Coach	Year(s)	Record
	1966	6-3-0
	1967	4-3-2
	1968	7-2-0
	1969	7-2-0
	1970	7-2-0 (SIAC Champions)
	1971	6-2-1 (SIAC Champions)
	1972	8-2-0 (SIAC Champions)
	1973	7-1-1
	1974	5-3-0
	1975	7-1-2
	1976	8-2-0 (SIAC Champions)
Leland Mangrum (2 years, 12-7-3)	1977	6-4-1
	1978	6-3-2
Douglas Porter (7 years, 57-17-2)	1979	5-3-1
	1980	7-3-1
	1981	9-2-0
	1982	10-2-0
	1983	9-1-0
	1984	8-3-0
	1985	9-3-0
Gerald Walker	1986	7-3-0
Douglas Porter (10 years, 56-48-1)	1987	5-5-0
	1988	5-5-0

Head Coach	Year(s)	Record
	1989	7-3-0
	1990	4-7-0
	1991	7-3-0
	1992	7-4-0
	1993	6-4-1
	1994	5-5-0
	1995	4-7-0
	1996	6-5-0
Kent Schoolfield (6 years, 42-27)	1997	5-6-0
	1998	11-2-0
	1999	10-2-0 (SIAC Champions)
	2000	7-4-0
	2001	8-3-0
	2002	1-10-0
John Morgan (3 years, 21-11)	2003	7-4-0
	2004	7-4-0
	2005	7-3-0
Deondri Clark (3 years, 18-15)	2006	4-7-0
	2007	8-3-0
	2008	6-5-0
Donald Pittman (3 years, 17-15)	2009	7-4-0
	2010	8-3-0
	2011	2-8-0

SIAC Division II Championships: 1982, 1983, 1985, 1991, 1992

> *1985: Two-Way Tie with Albany State*
> *1991: Five-Way Tie with Alabama A&M, Clark Atlanta, Morehouse and Tuskegee*

SHORTER COLLEGE

Head Coach	Year(s)	Record
Phil Jones (7 years, 26-33)	2005	3-7-0
	2006	7-4-0
	2007	7-4-0
	2008	9-3-0
	2009	6-5-0
	2010	5-6-0

SHORTER UNIVERSITY

Phil Jones (cont.)	2011	6-4-0

SAVANNAH STATE

GEORGIA INDUSTRIAL COLLEGE

Head Coach	Year(s)	Record
W.P. Tucker (6 years, 4-8)	1915	1-1-0

Head Coach	Year(s)	Record
	1923	1-0-0
	1925	1-0-0
	1926	0-1-0
	1927	1-3-0
	1928	0-3-0
Richard Richardson (6 years, 7-12-4)	1929	1-2-0
	1930	1-0-1
	1931	1-3-1
	1932	1-2-1
	1933	3-1-0
	1934	0-4-1
Arthur Dwight (5 years, 12-9-2)	1935	3-3-0
	1936	2-2-0
	1937	1-2-1

GEORGIA STATE COLLEGE

Arthur Dwight (cont.)	1938	3-2-0
	1939	3-0-1
W. McKinley King (2 years, 4-6-2)	1940	3-3-1
	1941	1-3-1
John H. Myles (2 years, 4-3-2)	1942	3-2-1
	1946	1-1-1

Head Coach	Year(s)	Record
Ted A. Wright (2 years, 6-8-1)	1947	1-5-1
	1948	5-3-0
John Martin (4 years, 12-21-2)	1949	3-5-0

SAVANNAH STATE COLLEGE

John Martin (cont.)	1950	3-4-1
	1951	5-4-1
	1952	1-8-0
Albert Frazier	1953	0-8-0
Ross Pearly (3 years, 7-15-1)	1954	1-7-0
	1955	2-4-1
	1956	4-4-0
Richard Washington (7 years, 22- 31-6)	1957	3-3-2
	1958	5-4-0
	1959	3-4-2
	1960	3-5-1
	1961	4-4-1
	1962	4-5-0
	1963	0-6-0
Leo Richardson (5 years, 13-25-2)	1964	1-6-0
	1965	1-6-1
	1966	3-5-0
	1967	6-2-1
	1968	2-6-0

Head Coach	Year(s)	Record
John H. Myles (8 years, 25-45-2)	1969	3-5-0
	1970	3-5-0
	1971	4-4-1
	1972	6-3-0
	1973	3-6-0
	1974	3-6-1
	1975	3-7-0
	1976	0-9-0
Frank Ellis Jr. (9 years, 33-55-2)	1977	4-5-0
	1978	4-6-0
	1979	6-3-1
	1980	5-5-0
	1981	4-6-0
	1982	4-5-0
	1983	2-9-0
	1984	2-7-1
	1985	2-9-0
William R. "Bill" Davis (7 years, 47-26)	1986	6-4-0
	1987	4-6-0
	1988	7-3-0
	1989	8-1-0
	1990	7-4-0
	1991	7-4-0
	1992	8-4-0
Joseph C. Crosby (2 years, 13-6-2)	1993	5-3-2

Head Coach	Year(s)	Record
	1994	8-3-0
Wendell Avery (2 years, 13-8)	1995	7-4-0

SAVANNAH STATE UNIVERSITY

Wendell Avery (cont.)	1996	6-4-0
Daryl McNeill (2 years, 10-12)	1997	3-8-0
	1998	7-4-0
Steve Wilks	1999	5-6-0
William R. "Bill" Davis (2 years, 4-15)	2000	2-8-0
	2001	2-7-0
Ken Pettiford (2 years, 1-14)	2002	1-9-0
	2003 (partial)	0-5-0
Richard Basil (3 years, 2-26)	2003 (partial)	0-7-0
	2004	2-8-0
	2005	0-11-0
Theo Lemon (2 years, 3-18)	2006	2-9-0
	2007	1-9-0
Robby Wells (2 years, 7-15)	2008	5-7-0
	2009	2-8-0
Julius Dixon	2010	1-10-0
Steve Davenport	2011	1-10-0

MERCER UNIVERSITY

Head Coach	Year(s)	Record
Dave Beggs	1892	1-2-0
George Stallings	1894	0-1-0
JD Winston	1896	0-2-1
George Saussy	1897	0-1-0
	1903	0-1-0
E.E. Tarr	1906	2-3-0
H.R. Schenker	1907	3-3-0
Frank Blake (2 years, 6-8)	1908	3-4-0
	1909	3-4-0
CC Stroud (4 years, 15-12-2)	1910	6-3-0
	1911	4-6-1
	1912	5-3-1
	1913	2-5-1
Fred A. Robins	1914	5-4-0
John Zellars	1915	5-4-0
John Zellars/D.R. Peacock	1916	1-6-0
Maxwell James	1919	0-2-0
Josh Cody (3 years, 10-19)	1920	2-7-0
	1921	3-6-0
	1922	5-6-0

Head Coach	Year(s)	Record
Stanley Robinson (3 years, 13-13-2)	1923	4-5-0
	1924	5-3-2
	1925	4-5-0
Bernie Moore (3 years, 12-12-3)	1926	4-3-1
	1927	5-4-0
	1928	3-5-1
Lake Russell (12 years, 46-60-6)	1929	2-6-1
	1930	5-5-0
	1931	7-2-1
	1932	7-2-0
	1933	4-3-2
	1934	3-6-1
	1935	4-5-0
	1936	3-6-1
	1937	4-5-0
	1938	3-6-0
	1939	3-7-0
	1940	1-7-0
Bobby Hooks	1941	3-6-0
(no coach)	1981	0-1-0
(no coach)	1982	0-2-0

MIDDLE GEORGIA COLLEGE

Head Coach	Year(s)	Record
	1934	0-2-0
	1935	0-2-0
	1936	0-1-0
	1937	1-0-0
	1938	0-1-0
	1939	1-0-0
	1940	0-1-0
	1941	0-1-0
	1957	2-0-0
	1958	1-0-0

Founded: 1923, played through 1959
Record: 54-18 from 1994 to 2000
Bowl Appearances/Wins: 4 appearances and 3 wins (2 Mineral Water Bowl wins)
   1995: 42–37 over Hutchinson (Kansas)
   1998: 41–3 over NW Mississippi
   1999: Golden Isles Bowl appearance

MORRIS BROWN COLLEGE

Head Coach	Year(s)	Record
	1996	0-4-0
	1997	3-2-0

Head Coach	Year(s)	Record
	1998	1-3-0
	1999	6-5-0
	2000	4-6-0 (SIAC)
	2001	5-6-0
	2002	1-11-0 (FCS Ind.)

OGLETHORPE UNIVERSITY

Head Coach	Year(s)	Record
Frank Anderson (3 years, 6-10-1)	1917	1-2-0
	1918	5-3-0
	1919	2-5-1
Walter Elcock (2 years, 9-7-1)	1920	4-3-1
	1921	5-4-0
Russel Stein	1922	1-9-0
Jim Robertson	1923	4-6-0
Harry Robertson (10 years, 39-47-5)	1924	6-3-1
	1925	8-3-0
	1926	3-6-1
	1927	2-6-0
	1928	3-5-1
	1929	5-4-1

Head Coach	Year(s)	Record
	1930	4-4-1
	1931	3-5-0
	1932	4-5-0
	1933	1-6-0
John Patrick (8 years, 20-32-1)	1934	5-4-1
	1935	2-7-0
	1936	4-5-0
	1937	0-2-0
	1938	0-4-0
	1939	0-1-0
	1940	2-6-0
	1941	3-3-0

LaGrange College

Head Coach	Year(s)	Record
Todd Mooney (6 years, 21-40)	2006	0-10-0
	2007	0-10-0
	2008	9-2-0 / 7-0-0 (SLIAC Champions/ NCAA Division III Playoff Participant)
	2009	5-5-0

Head Coach	Year(s)	Record
	2010	3-7-0
	2011	4-6-0

BREWTON-PARKER COLLEGE

The inaugural football season at Brewton-Parker Institute (it was an elementary/high boarding school back then) was in the fall of 1913. In 1929, after Brewton-Parker was elevated to junior college status, the team was named the Blue Barons to honor the Scottish heritage of the surrounding community. Football was discontinued in 1936 for ten years due to financial issues. In 1946, there was a final attempt to resurrect football at Brewton-Parker. Coach Franklin Ross Jones, working with very little scholarship money, was able to recruit some twenty-five players in the fall of 1946. He renamed the team the Squeaking Deacons, and they posted a 3-3-1 record that final season.

Thanks to Ann Hughes.

CLARK ATLANTA UNIVERSITY

Head Coach	Year(s)	Record
Sam Taylor	1925–29	22-9-4
Walter Aiken	1930–34	19-19-6
Ralph Robinson	1935–40	14-26-0

CLARK COLLEGE

Head Coach	Year(s)	Record
Ralph Robinson	1941–44	11-11-4
Coach McPherson	1945–47	10-9-2
Marion Curry	1948–50	10-10-2
Leonidas Epps	1951–69	70-71-9
Jessee Mclardy Sr.	1970–87	54-96-2

ATLANTA UNIVERSITY

William Spencer	1988–89	4-15-0
Willie Hunter	1990–96	20-31-0
Elmer Mixon	1997–99	7-18-0
Curtis Crockett	1999–2001	8-19-0
Tracey Hamm	2002–3	2-20-0
Trayrone Odums	2004	1-9-0
Ted Bauher	2005–2009	19-33-0
Daryl McNeill	2010–present	6-14-0

Overall Record	1925–2011	277-410-29
ALL-TIME RECORD	**1900–2011**	**278-429-29**

Name of School: Clark Atlanta University
Founded: 1988 (Consolidation of Atlanta University in 1865 and Clark College in 1869)
Nickname: Panthers
School Colors: Red, Black and Gray
Conference: Southern Intercollegiate Athletic Conference (SIAC)
First Year of NCAA Football: 1900
Conference Championships: 1928 and 1991

GEORGIA SOUTHWESTERN UNIVERSITY

Head Coach	Year(s)	Record
Jimmy Hightower (6 years, 26-24-1)	1983	5-4-0
	1984	5-3-0
	1985	5-3-0
	1986	5-4-0
	1987	4-3-1
	1988	2-7-0

REFERENCES

ARTICLES/PERIODICALS

Atlanta Journal-Constitution. "UGA President Adams Is Stepping Down." May 2, 2012. AJC.com.

Bowden, Terry. Article on Yahoo! Sports. June 15, 2008. Sports.Yahoo.com.

Chen, Albert. "Options All-Around." *Sports Illustrated*, November 16, 2009. SI.com.

Florence (AL) Times Daily, October 19, 1987.

Georgia Bulletin, October 4, 1979.

Higgins, Ron. "Herschel Never Stops Running." SEC Digital Network, April 23, 2012.

Houston Chronicle, December 26, 1995. chron.com.

Hudon, Paul Stephen. "Flight of the Stormy Petrel: The Glory Years of Oglethorpe University Athletics." *Atlanta History Magazine* (Summer 1992).

Jenkins, Dan. "It's Time to Bring On the Dogs." *Sports Illustrated*, November 21, 1966. SI.com.

Middle Georgia College Football Media Guide.

Murray Poole. "Bishop Continues to Enjoy Athletic Board Role." *Bulldawg Illustrated*, April 23, 2012.

OnlineAthens. "ND at Georgia Tech: The Other 'Rudy.'" September 2, 2006. OnlineAthens.com.

Reed, Thomas Walter. "History of the University of Georgia." Georgia Info. georgiainfo.galileo.usg.edu.

Rousos, Rick. "Bobby and His Boys." *Lakeland (FL) Ledger*, December 1, 2009.

Spartanburg (SC) Herald-Journal, January 25, 1964.

Sports Illustrated. "Great Run, Wrong Way." January 3, 1955. SI.com.

Stasny, Anthony. *Savannah News-Press*. August 24, 1990.

Sugiura, Ken. "Kennesaw State Plans to Field 2014 Football Team." *Atlanta Journal-Constitution*, September 15, 2010. AJC.com.

Taaffe, William. "A Big Day for the Small Fry." *Sports Illustrated*, October 11, 1982. SI.com.

Technique newspaper, 1997.

Thamel, Pete. "Grier Integrated a Game and Earned the World's Respect." *New York Times*, January 1, 2006. nytimes.com.

Wahl, Grant. "Morris Brown's Woes Worsen." *Sports Illustrated*, January 22, 2003. SI.com.

Wilmington (NC) Sunday Star News, September 16, 1984.

Wilmington Star-News, December 21, 1989.

Youngstown (OH) Vindicator. Vindy.com.

Books/Theses

King, Kim, and Jack Wilkinson. *Kim King's Tales from the Georgia Tech Sideline*. N.p.: Sports Publishing, LLC, 2004.

McMath, Robert C., and Ronald Bayor. *Engineering the New South: Georgia Tech 1885–1985*. Athens: University of Georgia Press, n.d.

Nelson, Jon. *Georgia High School Football: Peach State Pigskin History*. Charleston, SC: The History Press, 2011.

———. *100 Things Georgia Bulldog Fans Should Know and Do Before They Die*. N.p.: Triumph Books, 2010.

Patrick, John. "Football at Oglethorpe University: A History." Master's thesis. Oglethorpe University, May 15, 1935.

Wilder, Robert. *Gridiron Glory Days: Football at Mercer, 1892–1942*. Macon, GA: Mercer University Press, 2011.

RESOURCE WEBSITES

About Them Dawgs! patrickgarbin.blogspot.com.
Albany State University. asurams.edu.
Allstate Sugar Bowl. allstatesugarbowl.org.
Brewton-Parker College. bpc.edu.
Clark Atlanta Panthers. clarkatlantasports.com.
College Football Reference. cfreference.net.
Football Study Hall. footballstudyhall.com.
From the Rumble Seat—Georgia Tech Yellow Jacket Fans. fromtherumbleseat.com.
Georgia Military College. athletics.gmc.cc.ga.us.
Georgia Southern University Eagles Athletics. georgiasoutherneagles.com.
Georgia Southwestern University. gsw.edu.
Georgia State Athletics. georgiastatesports.com.
Georgia Tech Alumni Association. gtalumni.org.
Georgia Tech Athletics. ramblingwreck.com.
Gulf South Conference. gulfsouthconference.org/index.aspx.
HBCU Classic Sports. hbcuclassics.com.
LaGrange Athletics. lagrangepanthers.com.
LA84 Foundation. la84foundation.org.
Mercer University Athletics. mercerbears.com.
Middle Georgia College. mgc.edu.
Morehouse College Maroon Tigers. athletics.morehouse.edu.
Morris Brown College. morrisbrown.edu.
NCAA Division III Football. D3football.com.
New Georgia Encyclopedia. georgiaencyclopedia.org/nge/home.jsp.
Newnan Times-Herald. Times-Herald.com.
North Georgia News. accessnorthgeorgia.com.
Oglethorpe University. gopetrels.com.
Open Jurist. openjurist.org.
Orange Bowl. orangebowl.org.
Roll 'Bama Roll. rollbamaroll.com.
Savannah State University. ssuathletics.com.
The Savvy Sista. the-savvy-sista.com.
Shorter University. goshorterhawks.com/landing/index.
Southern Intercollegiate Athletic Conference. thesiac.com.
Sports Writers. sportswriters.net.
StingTalk—Georgia Tech Sports Message Board. stingtalk.com.

REFERENCES

University of Georgia Athletics. georgiadogs.com.
University of West Georgia. uwgsports.com.
Valdosta State. vstateblazers.com.
WRDW-TV News 12. WRDW.com.

ABOUT THE AUTHOR

J on Nelson has been a television journalist for more than twenty years, based in Atlanta. He graduated from Florida State University with a bachelor's of science degree in political science. His television career has given him the opportunity to cover events as varied as Super Bowls, World Series, All-Star Games, Summer Olympiads, the Masters, U.S. Opens, Grey Cups and even political conventions. He has also covered high school athletics for Georgia Public Broadcasting for seventeen years as a host, correspondent and sideline reporter/anchor.

Visit us at
www.historypress.net